Abbe Pichon

The life of Monseigneur Berneux

Bishop of Capse, vicar-apostolic of Corea

Abbe Pichon

The life of Monseigneur Berneux
Bishop of Capse, vicar-apostolic of Corea

ISBN/EAN: 9783741197673

Manufactured in Europe, USA, Canada, Australia, Japa

Cover: Foto ©Lupo / pixelio.de

Manufactured and distributed by brebook publishing software (www.brebook.com)

Abbe Pichon

The life of Monseigneur Berneux

THE LIFE

OF

MONSEIGNEUR BERNEUX,

BISHOP OF CAPSE, VICAR-APOSTOLIC OF CORBA.

By M. L'ABBÉ PICHON.

Translated from the French.

WITH A PREFACE BY LADY HERBERT.

LONDON:
BURNS, OATES, AND COMPANY,
Portman Street and Paternoster Row.
1872.

LONDON:
ROBSON AND SONS, PRINTERS, PANCRAS ROAD, N.W.

PREFACE.

'*In cœlo quies*' was a motto I once saw on a venerable Bishop's seal; and if ever there was a case in which this motto was applicable, it is in the beautiful life of labour and devotion which we are about to present in an English dress to our readers, to form part of the 'Missionary Series' published for the benefit of the new Foreign Missionary College at Mill Hill.

We have already recorded the virtues and triumphs of two other martyrs in the same land —Henri Dorié and Théophane Vénard; but they had laboured only a short time in their Lord's vineyard when they were called upon to receive their reward, one in Tonquin and one in the Corea. Mgr. Berneux, on the contrary, was spared to labour for twenty-six years on this soil, so full of hope and consolation to the eye of faith, but so full of trial and suffering to flesh and blood. On two separate occasions during that time he was put to the question, and tortured in a manner which one can scarcely bear to read: but it was not till worn out with incessant fatigues and superhuman privations, that his white head fell under the sword-thrusts of the persecutors. His letter describing (by command of his superiors) the first of these interrogations at Tonquin is (in the words of Mgr. de Carcassone, who pronounced Mgr. Berneux's funeral eulogy in his native place), 'one of the grandest and most touching pages in the history of the Church.'

Throughout, he seems to be fearful of robbing God of the honour which is His due, by attributing to himself the least of the extraordinary graces he received. God alone, indeed, could have given our poor human nature the strength and the courage to bear without a word an amount of physical agony, the very recital of which makes one shudder. The executioners being at last weary of tormenting him, he was thrown into a horrible dungeon, where he remained for months, exposed alternately to intense cold and heat, without shelter, without clothes, and nearly dying of hunger. What does he do during this time? He composes a hymn of praise, of which the 'refrain' is,

'Vive la joie toujours,
Vive la joie *quand même.*'

'*Hilarem datorem diligit Deus*'—God loves those who give themselves with joy. Such was eminently the spirit of this great servant of God. In Tonquin, in Mandchouria, and finally in the Corea, we see the same indomitable courage, the same burning zeal, the same ardent love for the salvation of souls: no fatigues, no physical suffering, no amount of privation of things which we are accustomed to look upon as mere necessaries of life, ever daunted his noble heart or caused him to relax for one instant from his arduous labours. And then the end came.

Nothing was to be lacking in the passion of this true disciple of Jesus Christ; not even the treachery of Judas, for he was betrayed by one of his own disciples whom he had trusted, and then dragged before the tribunals. Scourged, torn, and bruised, till his whole body was one wound, and then led to execution in the place reserved for the greatest malefactors; up to the last, his words were the same as his Master's. He has no feeling for his own sufferings; he weeps only for the poor pagans round him, for his poor flock, left as sheep without a shepherd; and when his bearers (for his legs had been broken in the torture, and he could not stand) paused for a moment on the way, his feeble voice still encouraged his fellow-martyrs in words full of joy and hope and love. As we read this deeply interesting narrative we are tempted over and over again to think, 'But this surely all happened long ago. Such horrors cannot take take place *now*.'

Alas, the world does not change. We need not go farther than Paris to see to what lengths even a civilised people can go when hounded on by the powers of darkness and filled with hatred of God and of His servants. It was in 1866—only six short years ago—that this terrible scene of martyrdom was enacted in the Corea. Perhaps at this very moment similar tortures are being borne for the faith in those distant lands; for if the world does not change, still less does the Church of God. In vain do the rulers rage, and the people imagine a vain thing. Jesus Christ is King. His reign will be established upon earth in spite of all the powers of earth and hell. The times and the seasons are in God's own hands. All we have to do is to labour, each one in his own sphere, to promote His glory and to save souls. With such examples before us, can we be idle and hold back?

MARY ELIZABETH HERBERT.

Wilton, Nov. 1872.

EXTRACT FROM THE AUTHOR'S PREFACE.

IT was in September of the year 1866 that the news reached Paris of the martyrdom of the two Bishops and seven Catholic missionaries of the Corea. The pupils of the 'Séminaire des Missions Etrangères,' many of whom were destined ere long to fill up the vacant places of those who had thus gloriously fallen, being at that time in the country, at once, and with an enthusiasm worthy of their high vocation, improvised an illumination amongst the trees overshadowing the statue of our Blessed Lady, whilst they sang a *Te Deum* as an act of thanksgiving, with invocations to the Queen and Mother of Martyrs.

Thus were inaugurated those holy rejoicings, by which, in the birthplace of each of our sainted martyrs, the new triumphs of the Holy Catholic Church were soon to be celebrated. For as Saint Leo says : ' No cruelty, however barbarous, can destroy the religion founded upon the Cross of Christ. Persecution cannot enfeeble the Church, but will most surely strengthen her; and the field of the Lord, like the grain, which, sown singly, multiplies a hundredfold, will bear a countless harvest where the seed falls one by one.' 'Nec ullo crudelitatis genere destrui potest sacramento crucis Christi fundata religio. Non minuitur persecutionibus Ecclesia, sed augetur; et semper dominicus ager segete, ditiori vestitur, dum grana, quæ singula cadunt, multiplicatur nascuntur' (*Serm.* 8° *in Natali Apost. Petri et Pauli*).

It is reserved for the Holy See of St. Peter alone to pronounce upon the martyrdom or beatification of the Church's saints. It is with no intention therefore of infringing upon a reserve so necessary to the discipline of the Church that we give, as we not unfrequently do in the course of this narrative, the title of 'saint' and 'martyr' to Mgr. Berneux and other missionaries. Nevertheless, we feel, as the Bishop of Poictiers remarked on the occasion of the anniversary of the death of M. Théophane Vénard, martyr of Tonquin, 'there are cases so evident, that they carry conviction along with them.' And such is the one before us. No one can dispute the fact that our fellow-citizen is a martyr; and to know him by the title which a glorious death for the faith has won for him, is simply the highest panegyric that can be pronounced upon him. 'Appelavi martyrem, predicavi satis.' (St. Ambrose, *Lib. de Virg.*)

CONTENTS.

CHAPTER I.

His early years. Account given by M. Nouard. His entrance into the great Seminary of Mans. Tutor in the families of Carron and De la Bonillerie. Letters to his pupil. Desire to enter the monastic life. He is drawn towards the priesthood; is ordained deacon in 1836 at the age of 22, and enters the priesthood in 1837. Is made Professor of Theology in 1838. Discovers his vocation . . . . *Page* 1

CHAPTER II.

The Seminary des Missions Etrangères. Manner of life. Martyrdoms in Tonquin. M. Berneux prepares for his departure. Has charge of a community in the mean time. Separation from his mother. Sudden departure. Writes from Havre 19th January 1842 . . *p.* 11

CHAPTER III.

The voyage. Arrival at Anjer. Thoughts on passing the shores of Cochin-China. Arrival at Manilla. Mgr. Retord. Departure for Macao . . . . *p.* 18

CHAPTER IV.

Arrival at Macao. Importance of this place. Meets M. Taillandier. Adopts Chinese customs and costume. Departure and capture of M. Taillandier. Captivity and release. Mgr. Retord takes M. Berneux. Their departure for Tonquin is fixed . . . *p.* 23

CONTENTS.

CHAPTER V.

Passage to Tonquin. Arrival. Death of Minh-Mênh. Missionaries separate. M. Berneux is left in hiding in a convent . . . . *p.* 30

CHAPTER VI.

Tonquin. Brief summary of its geographical position, and the history of the Church during the 240 years of its existence. Hopes entertained at the commencement of the present century. Successful negotiations on the part of the Vicar-apostolic of Cochin-China with the King of France to restore Gia Laong to the throne. Ingratitude of this monarch. His death, and the cruel reign of his son Minh-Mênh . . . . . *p.* 36

CHAPTER VII.

Discovery of MM. Galy and Berneux. They are taken prisoners, and put in cages. Conduct of neophytes and Christians. Imprisonment at Nam-Dinh. Examinations. Departure for and journey to Hué. Arrival. *p.* 42

CHAPTER VIII.

Examinations at Hué. Missionaries commanded to dishonour the Cross. They refuse, and are put to the torture. They are insulted both in their prisons and in the streets. They are found guilty of preaching the Gospel, and condemned to death . . . *p.* 57

CHAPTER IX.

Arrest of MM. Charrier, Miche, and Duclos. Miseries of the captivity. Christian sympathy. Confessors of Quang-tri. Visit of Philip Phê. Sentence of death; joy of the missionaries. Death-warrant signed, and missionaries removed to the great prison. Execution indefinitely postponed. Description of the prison. Horrors of this captivity . . . . *p.* 66

CONTENTS. xi

CHAPTER X.

Their delivery by the prompt and bold measures taken by M. Lévêque, commander of the Héroïne. They are taken on board the Héroïne, and set sail for France. MM. Miche and Duclos are left at Singapore . . *p.* 76

CHAPTER XI.

Voyage to Bourbon. M. Berneux obtains permission from the governor to return to Macao. He is appointed to Mandchouria. Journey and arrival . . *p.* 80

CHAPTER XII.

Mandchouria. Divisions: 1. Ghirin-Oula. 2. Sakhalien. 3. Leao-Tong. Climate. Poverty. Chinese element. Religions. Superstitions . . . . *p.* 85

CHAPTER XIII.

Commencement of missionary labours in Mandchouria. Account of M. Berneux's manner of teaching . *p.* 92

CHAPTER XIV.

Threatening persecution. Prompt measures taken by the Bishop and M. Berneux. Peace is restored. He is raised to the Episcopate, and appointed Vicar-apostolic of the Corea . . . . *p.* 98

CHAPTER XV.

Corea. Christianity introduced by the Japanese about the end of the sixteenth century. Success. The faith proclaimed publicly even before the arrival of a priest. First persecution. The first missionary, a young Chinese priest, gives himself up in 1801. Mgr. Bruguière offers himself (1833) for the work: his death two years after . . . . *p.* 104

CHAPTER XVI.

In 1839 Mgr. Imbert gives himself up with his priests to death. The family Tschoez. Mgr. Ferréol in 1845: illness and death in 1853. Mgr. Berneux . *p.* 109

CHAPTER XVII.

Short description of Corea. Corean race. Government. Classes. Dwellings. Customs in mourning. Food. Privations . . . . *p.* 117

CHAPTER XVIII.

Mgr. Berneux fixes his residence in the capital. Method of administration. Great precautions. Interesting details. Faith and fervour of the Christians: their heroism and power of endurance. Consecration of M. Daveluy as coadjutor Bishop of Acônes . . . . *p.* 125

CHAPTER XIX.

Difficulties of missionary work. Printing. Baptism of infants in danger of death. Work of the 'Holy Infancy.' Native clergy. Foundation of two colleges: the movement begins to be general: hopes brighten. Fresh persecutions in 1860. Cholera and famine. Two printing-presses are set up. Slow but gradual development of the mission . . . . . . *p.* 137

CHAPTER XX.

Character of Mgr. Berneux. His extraordinary activity and self-denial. His tenderness and care of his missionaries. Their unbounded love and respect . . *p.* 147

CHAPTER XXI.

Death of the king in 1864. Change affects the prospects of the mission. Presence of missionaries known to the authorities. Last letter of Mgr. Berneux to his friends. Demand of Russia for a concession of territory. The Bishops are called upon to mediate. Their mediation subsequently refused. Arrest, trial, and death of the missionaries. Conclusion . . . . *p.* 152

THE LIFE

OF

MONSEIGNEUR BERNEUX,

BISHOP AND MARTYR.

CHAPTER I.

His early years. Account given by M. Nouard. His entrance into the great Seminary of Mans. Tutor in the families of Carron and De la Bouillerie. Letters to his pupil. Desire to enter the monastic life. He is drawn towards the priesthood; is ordained deacon in 1836 at the age of 22, and enters the priesthood in 1837. Is made Professor of Theology in 1838. Discovers his vocation.

SIMEON FRANÇOIS BERNEUX, Bishop of Capse *in partibus infidelium*, Vicar-apostolic of the Corea, who, on the 8th March 1866, was beheaded for the faith, was born May 14th, 1814, in the town of Château-sur-Loir, in the diocese of Mans, of humble but religious parents.

It is from M. l'Abbé Nouard, now *Curé-Doyen* of Couptrain (who, as Vicar of Château-sur-Loir during the childhood of M. Berneux, discovered and fostered the early vocation of our holy martyr), that we have been happy enough to collect many interesting details of his early life. 'When,' he writes, 'I first entered upon my charge at Château-sur-Loir, in 1824, I found a boy ten years of age, the child of poor but industrious parents, with whose appearance I was struck as indicative of a remarkably excellent disposition. I made him one of my choirboys, where he soon became, from his good conduct, an example to all the rest. Soon after he expressed a great desire to study for the priesthood; I therefore gave him some lessons; but, for lack of time to instruct him myself, I placed him in the little college of Château-sur-Loir, where he soon distinguished himself by the regularity of his conduct and his rapid progress. At catechism he was so far superior to the others, that I habitually made him hear the lesson, whilst I merely superintended and explained. I do not believe he was ever rallied by his young companions on this account, as they all respected him too much. From thence he went to the college of Mans; and in order to avoid the dangers to which boys are exposed who come from little seminaries, he begged to be allowed to be sent instead to that of Précigné, to which I consented.'

It was at Précigné that he made the acquaintance of a younger fellow-student, one who was destined eventually to rule the church of Mans. In his beautiful pastoral announcing a solemn thanksgiving on the event of the martyrdom of Mgr. Berneux, Mgr. Fillion gives the following touching tribute to his memory:

'Were we about to place before you a sketch of the life of this servant of God, it would be a real satisfaction to gather together the recollections of a long and precious friendship, and to picture him to you as we ourselves have known him in the little seminary of Précigné, as a model of all virtuous scholars from his piety, regularity, and studiousness; or at St. Vincent as an ornament of the diaconate, holding as distinguished a place in the esteem of the masters as in the affection of his fellow-students, not one of whom has expressed surprise at the great things which he has achieved.'

In 1831 M. Berneux entered the great seminary. Being but seventeen years of age, too young as yet to be admitted to holy orders, and his health having suffered from excess of work, he was permitted to take a little rest from his studies, and placed as tutor in the family of M. Carron, cousin of M. Bouvier, Bishop of Mans, and later on, in that of M. de la Bouillerie. Although but six months an inmate of M. Carron's house, the greatest friendship was contracted between him and his pupil, who frequently visited him during his subsequent residence in the Séminaire des Missions Etrangères. His engagement with the family of M. de la Bouillerie was of longer standing, and the intimacy which he formed with the different members of this family, and especially with M. Henri de la Bouillerie, his pupil, was one which neither time nor separation could diminish. But in order to form some idea of him during this period of his life, we cannot do better than quote the words of Mgr. de la Carcassonne, brother of M. Henri de la Bouillerie:

'It is more particularly,' said he, 'when a person becomes an inmate of your home that you learn to know him as he really is. It is by our own fireside that your holy missionary has sat: goodness, piety, gentle gaiety, the noblest qualities of mind and of heart, all that can inspire a child with the taste for study and a love of prayer, all were found united in him. The letters which he wrote to his pupil we have carefully preserved; and now that a rich diadem encircles his brow, these are no longer merely bright and holy recollections, they speak of one who is our glory and our pride. It was then that I first knew him personally: tall of stature, with a slight stoop, and, as far as I can recollect, with a countenance expressive of the greatest sweetness and gentleness, he drew all hearts towards him.'

M. Berneux returned to the Seminary of Mans in October 1834, at the age of twenty, in order to finish his theological studies; but he continued to keep up a close correspondence with his pupil M. Henri de la Bouillerie, thus revealing his inner life in a way which renders these letters specially valuable as the outpourings of the heart of the future apostle and martyr.

In May 1835 he writes thus:

'I am very glad to find you have not forgotten me, and that you like to recall the many walks we took together. I assure you, dearest child, I often think of La Flèche, of the games of draughts you lost there, of the walks at La Barbée on Thursdays, and of your little sorrowful face when you were kept in to finish a task. Very often I travel in thought from Paris to Croissy, from la Rue Cassette to Vaugirard. Then come the Pyrenees, our rides in the early morning to the little fountain, and at last our sorrowful separation. O my child, how many recollections have we not together, at once sweet yet sorrowful!'

In order to encourage his pupil to greater diligence, he offers him his own example, by which we become acquainted with some details of his own studies.

'Although I am very busy, you are always in my thoughts. I am following up three courses of study at a time: physic, ecclesiastical history, and the Fathers of the Church; and I believe I shall continue to learn German. The professor of dogmatic theology works hard with me; nevertheless I have always time to think of you. Do not imagine that it is irksome to work hard; if you once really give it a trial, you will find a pleasure in it, and there are many reasons to induce you to persevere. Above all, there is the wish of pleasing God. Neglect of duty, of whatever nature, offends Him. And then your mother, dear child, it would make her so happy to see you what is called a good scholar! You cannot imagine how much she loves you.'

The letters which follow are a precious memorial of the piety of M. Berneux, and of the fervent desire he had to inspire his pupil with those feelings of faith and devotion which became his strength and consolation in after-life. He writes:

'Do not omit a single day to make a visit to the Blessed Sacrament, if it is but for five minutes. Get the habit of it at any cost. You will find the benefit of it by and by. Frequent Communion seems to frighten you. Why? It is true, that if we only considered our own miserable sins and weaknesses, we should never dare approach the holy table. But after we have made the best preparation we can, we must throw ourselves on the goodness and mercy of God, and believe that He will supply what is wanting in us. I only wish I could tell you, dear child, all the consolations which I find in Holy Communion, and especially during this last month, when a time of greater quiet has enabled me to receive it several times a week. . . . Do not give way to melancholy; it can only separate you farther from God. Reject all such thoughts as so many snares of the devil. Go on simply and humbly, dear child; have entire confidence in God: He is our best friend; and after that, have no farther disquiet. Every day I pray for you, and in fact many times in the day. I pray that God may fill you with His grace. Pray for me also, that I may obtain the virtues of which I stand so greatly in need.'

In this same letter, dated 5th Nov. 1835, he mentions the inclination he had had to enter the Benedictine Order at Solesmes; but impediments having been thrown in the way, and being drawn by God to the desire of greater perfection, and to work more especially for the salvation of souls, he attached himself to M. l'Abbé Moreau, assistant superior of the seminary, who was then endeavouring to form a society of priests who should live in community for the purpose of evangelising the diocese. Although he did not join this society, he was, singularly enough, ordained deacon in the church of the priory, now the abbey of the Benedictines of Solesmes, on the 24th September 1836. During the years 1836 and 1837 he was appointed assistant-teacher of philosophy at the great seminary; which was the more remarkable on account of his extreme youth. By his earnest desire, as soon as his age permitted it, he was ordained priest. His ordination took place on the 20th May 1837, in the Bishop's private chapel. By his permission the next twelve months were passed with M. Nouard, in order to recruit his health, which had suffered from excessive study and work; but in October 1838 the Bishop of Mans placed him as Professor of Theology at the great seminary.

It was during this year that he realised his vocation; and his desire to offer himself for the work of an apostle to the heathen was so great, that his health gave way under it. He confided his secret to M. Nouard, who had great difficulty in obtaining the Bishop's consent to this change in his plans; but perceiving that the pressing nature of the call he had received from God had materially affected his health, he at length permitted him to resign his post.

Natural ties and affections, however, had a very strong hold on the heart of this devoted servant of

God. His mother, to whom his resolve would probably be a death-blow, had but lately become a widow. To her he was tenderly attached; and all his correspondence at this period is full of touching expressions, which, while they reveal the struggle of nature with grace, are evidently permitted to escape him rather for the purpose of strengthening others to bear their share in the sacrifice, than as an indulgence to himself. He quitted Château-sur-Loir on the 1st July 1839, under the pretext of going to pass some days with M. Nouard. He had said nothing to his family about his vocation. 'O! how full my heart was,' he writes to his mother, 'when I said good-bye that night! I was so afraid you would suspect something. But I could not bear the thought of not seeing you once more.' It was, in fact, the last time he saw her on earth. At that moment he pressed her so warmly to his heart, and covered her so with kisses, that the poor mother was quite astonished. He seemed as if he could not tear himself from her. Alas! she knew the cause too well a little later: and his letter announcing his determination, and written from the Foreign Missionary College on the 27th July, although most tenderly and considerately worded, filled her with utter despair. A few days after, he wrote again to her: 'God is my witness, that to save you from this sorrow, I would willingly shed the last drop of my blood. There is but one sacrifice I cannot make. I dare not sacrifice my soul. I must fulfil the will of God. And you would not desire it! You would, I know, rather see me dead a thousand times than permit me to be unfaithful to my vocation. For if the separation of a few years be so great a grief to us, what would it not be to be parted for ever! Let us offer the bitter sorrow we feel to our good God, and He will soften it, and help us to bear it. And as for me, it will double the weight I already bear if you continue to grieve so much!'

Again to his sister he writes: 'God knows how dear you are to me! Life far away from you would be desolate indeed, if it were not for God's sake. He will sustain me wherever I go. He will be your support also. He will care for you as I cannot. Farewell, dearest sister. In this one thing we can ever be united—in the love and the service of God; and in this alone shall we find peace and happiness both here and hereafter.'

It was in this manner that M. Berneux endeavoured to prepare each member of his family for the cruel separation which would cost him so dear. But although called upon to exercise the most perfect detachment, he never relaxed through life a correspondence which bears witness to an unchanging affection for those whom God had given Him, whilst he did not cease to be their support and example under all their trials, and to share with ready sympathy in all their joys.

In order to obtain for his mother the courage and strength necessary in so keen a trial, he had asked for prayers from all the holiest souls he knew on her behalf. These prayers were apparently granted; for on the 25th of August he writes to her :

'What has filled me with joy in your last letter is the assurance that you have accepted the sacrifice which God has required of us, and are no longer so broken-hearted at my departure. Blessed be the God of all mercies and consolations, who has deigned to spare me from farther sorrow on this account! Your despair, my dearest mother, filled my heart with misery and bitterness. Now I feel a great peace, an untold consolation. Only think a moment, dearest mother! This vocation of mine—this glorious mission to carry the Gospel tidings to a people who know not God—this vocation, which worldly people, who think only of this life, look upon as the greatest misfortune both for you and for me, is in reality the source of untold blessings to us both. Our faith has become more vivid, our confidence in God stronger, our love for Him more ardent. I never cease to thank God for the way in which He has thus showered His graces upon us.... You say that your favourite meditation now is on the wounds of our dear Lord. I am so glad of it, for I feel that in no other way will you so readily learn conformity to His will. Following the example of the Blessed Virgin, dearest mother, you will offer your sacrifice not only with courage and resignation, but with joy, when you think of the high honour God has granted me, in spite of my unworthiness, of being permitted to work for the sanctification of the souls whom He died to save.'

We should have liked to have given further extracts from these beautiful letters, but we must hurry on to the more important part of his life.

CHAPTER II.

The Seminary des Missions Etrangerès. Manner of life. Martyrdoms in Tonquin. M. Berneux prepares for his departure. Has charge of a community in the mean time. Separation from his mother. Sudden departure. Writes from Havre 19th January 1842.

THE Seminary des Missions Etrangères at Paris, into which M. l'Abhé Berneux had just entered, was founded in 1657 for the purpose of receiving such ecclesiastics as are desirous of devoting themselves to missionary labour, whether amongst the heathen in distant countries, or amongst those who are separated by heresy or by schism from the Church. All who enter the seminary begin by the study of their particular vocation. The higher it proves to be, the more absolutely necessary it is that it should be carefully developed and well tried; and in this holy house, where everything is calculated to keep in remembrance the glorious example of the apostles and martyrs who have gone before, the missionary and martyr is prepared and formed to those sacerdotal virtues which make the true missionary. M. Berneux, speaking of the life at the seminary, writes thus:

'Our manner of life differs little from that of other seminaries, except in this, that we have more liberty, less study, and more time to devote to prayer and meditation. Truly, a missionary, if he would not lose the treasure of grace intrusted to him, ought to be a saint of no ordinary type.

'It should not indeed be impossible, or even difficult, to attain to such sanctity, considering the circumstances surrounding our lives. Examples, conversations, advice, prayers, nothing is wanting here to supernaturalise us. But the difficulty really lies in the individual heart of each; and it is there, alas, that grace finds the resistance which hinders the operations of the Holy Spirit. Such is precisely my case. Although at times I seem to have no desire but to do the will of God, nevertheless I am often one of those whom St. Stephen reproached by saying, "Ye do always resist the Holy Ghost." Let me beg of you, then, to assist me by your prayers, that I may yet receive that most important of God's favours—the grace to use grace. I hope to obtain it; for it is impossible that the prayers of so many holy souls who take so great an interest in my perfection should fail of being heard.'

Ecclesiastics who have not yet finished their theological studies complete them at the Seminary des Missions Etrangères, where they still remain for a little time afterwards, before being sent upon a mission. But this prolongation was not necessary in the case of M. Berneux, who had completed his with such honourable distinction at the Seminary of Mans, and was at once ready for any call. It was just at this time that news arrived of the glorious martyrdom of many members of their society at

Tonquin. Fifteen priests and two Bishops had been put to death, while a third Bishop had died of fatigue, suffering, and grief in flying from the persecution. Fresh labourers were therefore urgently wanted to repair the ravages in this desolate mission; and M. Berneux, though absolutely conformed to the will of God, could not help indulging the hope and the noble ambition of being chosen for a post so dear to the heart of every missionary, who, as a recompense for his devotion, is prepared to accept the crown of martyrdom.

Whilst awaiting his departure, his superiors placed a little community under his charge. There are many such in Paris, who have not a chaplain of their own, and the Seminary des Missions Etrangères allows its priests to say Mass for them and to give instructions. It is interesting to observe the perfect detachment which enabled him to throw himself into a temporary charge, as though he had no other vocation or more absorbing interest to occupy his heart. In a letter to M. Nouard upon the subject he writes: 'I have to say Mass and catechise the children and preach also, though after the manner of a poor little missionary. I am forbidden to give more than an hour to prepare myself, and I observe the injunction under the conviction that obedience is more profitable to myself and my hearers than the most highly-finished discourse. There is certainly but little room for vainglory, but provided we preach our Lord Jesus Christ, what more is necessary? It is very possible for man to speak foolishly, but God can make use of the humblest efforts to advance His glory and

to touch the hearts of men. I bless Him indeed
for having given me this charge. In it I can see
His loving care for His *spoiled child*. Amongst
these little ones' (an orphanage was attached to the
community) 'I find constant food for edification.
Their modest piety, the desire so many express for
death, in order to be once more united to Him whom
they love best—what a grace all this is for me!
May I too be enabled to nourish in the hearts of
these little ones a fervent love for Jesus Christ!'

On November 28, 1839, he announced to M.
Nouard the joyful news of his approaching departure,
together with two other young priests. 'God be
praised,' he exclaims, 'our vessel is at Havre. It
will take us direct to Macao, where the superior of
our missions there will assign to each of us our particular post. If the persecution in Cochin-China
or Tonquin should relax, we shall be sent there, in
order to repair the damages done in our Lord's vineyard. If not, we shall go either to Tartary, China,
or the Corea. O, how glorious is the portion which
God has assigned to me! Ere long perhaps I shall
tread the very soil where the blood of martyrs is yet
flowing! a land where everything preaches a lesson
of sanctity! O, what a grace is this for me, to help
me to overcome the evil that is in me! May I profit by it indeed, for the glory of God and the salvation of souls!

'I must set to work at once to become a Chinese. It will be hard work: I must learn to eat rice,
drink tea, smoke a pipe, shave my head, wear a pig-
tail, and a long beard as well, if it will grow! But

what matters? were it necessary to walk with head downwards and one's feet in the air, I am ready for all, provided it be for the glory of God!'

At the conclusion of this letter, M. Berneux begs his friend to conceal from his mother that his departure would take place so soon. It was her intention to come to Paris to try to change her son's resolution. However, she abandoned the idea, but begged that he would come home for the last time and bid them good-bye. His reply is characteristic:

'You ask me, my dearest mother, whether I shall come and see you before starting? I answer, that when I came to Paris, I resolved to obey my superior implicitly. If he permits me, I will come; if he does not, I shall submit. I thank you much for not coming to Paris. I could hardly have borne the separation afterwards; it would have been all the more painful for us both. I feel sure you would not wish to reopen the wound in my heart.'

As it happened, they did not meet again; for he was sent off very suddenly at last; but in order to compensate to his mother as much as possible for the pain which this must have caused her, he sent her his portrait with the following letter, which reveals his whole soul:

'Do not take this too much to heart, my dearest mother; it has not happened through any negligence on my part that I do not come to see you for the last time; and my portrait, which I send you, will prove how gladly I would, if I could, do something to soften your grief. I thought it would make you happy to have before you the likeness of the son whom you love so tenderly, and who would gladly give his life, if it were necessary, to insure your happiness—who would even sacrifice his vocation, if his conscience and the will of God permitted it. Put this portrait in your room, rather high up; look at it often and think of me, and pray the Mother of God to help us ever to do more and more the holy will of God. O, it is such a happiness to will that alone which God wills! Never has my soul known such peace. Nothing would be wanting to me, did I but know that you and my sister and her husband would resign yourselves to this sacrifice. I feel confident that you will do so. Is not the salvation of the soul the one thing needful? and shall we not find it? I, in carrying help to these perishing souls; and you, in offering this sacrifice of your son to God.'

He was obliged also to forego the pleasure of seeing M. Nouard, who had been instrumental in determining his vocation. 'I foresaw,' he writes, 'that it would be impossible for you to come and bless me before my departure; consequently your letter has grieved but not surprised me. It is nevertheless natural to hope for what we greatly desire; but doubtless God has ordered all these things for my good. He would have my sacrifice more perfect; and would teach me greater detachment from self, so as to desire and to seek in all nothing but His adorable will. I am certain that there can be no peace without this; and for a missionary, above all, who does not desire his labour to be without fruit, such a condition is absolutely necessary.

My poor mother still flatters herself that I shall be able to come and see her once more; but she is wonderfully resigned. Mary has helped her in this. I had implored this Consoler of the afflicted to soften my dear mother's sorrow, and you see she has not disdained my petition.'

On the 19th January 1840 he writes thus from Havre:

'We arrived here four days ago, and hope to sail on the 22d, weather permitting. The vessel is said to be a good sailer; we have each a little cabin on deck; so that, as far as our bodily wants are concerned, we are well provided for: may it please God to have the same care for our souls! Until now I have lived in the midst of plenty; the Bread of Heaven has never failed me; now will come a time of famine. I cannot help fearing that being no longer watered by the Precious Blood, my soul may become empty and barren, like the soil which the dew does not refresh. Deeply shall I feel this privation. Nevertheless I put my trust in God, and say, *Tuus sum ego: salvum me fac.* I hope in Him, and shall not be confounded.

'I am in perfect peace. I have not the least doubt about my vocation, since those whom God has appointed to determine it have decided that I am called to the apostolate. Therefore nothing terrifies me; and unless counter-ordered, were it with the certainty of being dashed the next moment against the rocks, I should not hesitate for a moment to embark.'

CHAPTER III.

The voyage. Arrival at Anjer. Thoughts on passing the shores of Cochin-China. Arrival at Manilla. Mgr. Retord. Departure for Macao.

A PROVIDENTIAL delay saved the party from such a catastrophe as the one alluded to in his last letter. Furious gales having sprung up, it was not until the 12th February that the weather permitted them to sail.

After a tolerably fair voyage, during which M. Berneux suffered for five weeks from incessant sea-sickness, they arrived at the Straits of Sunda on the 25th of May; and on the 11th of July he gives some interesting details of his voyage to M. Nouard:

'On Easter-day I was able to celebrate Holy Mass, the only time that I have had this happiness during four months and a half. On the 31st May we arrived at Anjer, in the island of Java. For three months and a half we had not set foot upon land; it was therefore very pleasant to have a rest there of six days. Anjer is a very considerable but poor village, and with the exception of a few tolerably well-built houses, it consists of miserable bamboo huts. The consul received us as brothers; but what the missionary most desires, especially after a long voyage, was not to be found. Not a single church in which we could celebrate the Holy Mysteries! not a single cross in this land of unbelievers! I regretted much being unable to make myself understood of these poor Mahometans, nor to be able to speak to them of our Lord Jesus Christ and of our holy religion. Who knows whether such seed, scattered as it were by chance, might not have produced some fruit?

'On the 19th of June we saw in the distance the coast of Cochin-China. I cannot express the feelings which stirred my soul at the sight of this soil, upon which so much blood has flowed that is dear to our Lord. Perhaps, I thought, at the very moment my eyes are resting on such or such a spot, one of my brethren is hiding himself from the persecution in some cave or other, or is confessing the faith amidst horrible tortures.'

It must be understood that the missionaries could not land on the coast of Cochin-China, on account of the cruel persecution which at that time raged there. They were obliged to continue their voyage towards the Philippine Islands, which, belonging to Spain, offered them safe shelter until such time as they should be able to cross over to China.

'On the 26th of June,' writes M. Berneux, 'we arrived at Manilla, where once more we found our Altar and our God. This is our time of abundance. We found here Mgr. Retord, Vicar-apostolic of Tonquin, who has come here to receive episcopal consecration; the persecution having cut down all our Bishops. As yet it continues as fierce as ever; but against hope I am hoping to be able to accompany Mgr. Retord to Tonquin.'

The reception of the missionaries at Manilla was of the most hearty description. The venerable Archbishop sent one of his priests on board, to conduct them to his house, and for six weeks they enjoyed the rest and the hospitality thus afforded them. Nevertheless M. Berneux looked upon the delay with a kind of holy jealousy, and longed to be at his post, and in the midst of the battle for souls. Of the Philippine Islands themselves he speaks thus:

'The Philippine Islands are one of the finest of the Spanish colonies. The aborigines or Tagals are converts to the Catholic faith, which is the only religion practised in these islands. Nevertheless some few savage and ferocious pagans still haunt the mountains, and the work of conversion, when attempted to be carried on amongst them, is attended with many difficulties.

'The churches in Manilla are very beautiful and richly decorated. The altars are all of massive silver, and the statues of the Blessed Virgin are enriched with wonderful jewels. The faith of the people is very fervent. Every house has its oratory; and when the Angelus sounds in the evening, every soul stops to salute the Mother of God. . . .'

After describing the dress of the natives, Mgr. Berneux continues:

'The one passion of the Tagals is cock-fighting. Every Tagal has his cock, which is more loved and petted than any other creature in the house. . . . . The first thing offered to you when you pay a visit to any one is chocolate, the next a cigar. Every one smokes, men, women, and children; and I have seen some women with cigars as big as carrots! You would have been very much astonished to see the Bishop of Tonquin, in his rochet and stole, accompanied by all the French missionaries, going in state to pay a visit to the Archbishop the other day, and having, as well as all the priests, a huge cigar in his mouth! But in Manilla a cigar seems to be looked upon as an integral part of the body.'

His farther accounts of the condition of the people generally, and of their ardent faith, are very interesting; but as they are not, strictly speaking, connected with the life of our missionary and martyr, we pass on to his more personal narrative.

Immediately on his arrival, M. Berneux, with characteristic energy, abandoned all European customs, and began to live like the natives.

'They wished,' he writes, 'to give us bread, being strangers; but upon this point I have become an Indian. I eat rice like a Tagal, and am in boisterous health. I know not what the meat is that is placed before me; it is sufficient that it appeases hunger.' He adds, speaking of certain customs somewhat contrary to our ideas of cleanliness: 'I have said once for all, that nothing *is* dirty, and therefore nothing disgusts me. I have found myself dining among Indians, and I have always done justice to my entertainer.'

Doubtless these are but trifles, yet greater courage is often required to accept little inconveniences with generosity than to bear more severe sufferings.

On the 31st of September he writes for the last time from Manilla:

'It seems that we shall certainly leave this the day after to-morrow. The weather is very fine, and our voyage will be short and agreeable. Last week I made a retreat with one of my companions at a country-house belonging to the University of Manilla. This house stands by itself on the sea-shore. Here we spent a delicious week. It was a wonderful rest after the distractions of the life we have been obliged to lead here; and it enabled us to prepare ourselves better for the apostolic ministry which we are about to exercise.

'My health is wonderful, notwithstanding the excessive heat. The rains have ceased during the last week, and the sun is scorching. My companions, who were robust in Europe, are all more or less affected by it. But I, whose health was so weak, am able to bear everything. Bless God for it, my dearest sister, from whose Hand we receive all these blessings.'

CHAPTER IV.

Arrival at Macao. Importance of this place. Meets M. Taillandier. Adopts Chinese customs and costume. Departure and capture of M. Taillandier. Captivity and release. Mgr. Retord takes M. Berneux. Their departure for Tonquin is fixed.

In consequence of the commercial difficulties existing at that time, owing to the war between England and China, M. Berneux and the other missionaries did not embark with Mgr. Retord for Macao. They followed him in the month of September, about six weeks afterwards.

Macao has been in possession of the Portuguese since the year 1580. But although masters by right, they are far from being masters in fact; and the Chinese mandarin who has charge of the police and of the interests of his fellow-countrymen, has much more power than the Portuguese. Before the war with England, and the consequent opening of several ports to European commerce, Macao was one of the principal centres of trade with China. The Society of the Missions Etrangères maintained an agent there to receive their missionaries, and to facilitate their entrance into the interior of China. Their letters and supplies of money also passed through his hands. But Macao is by no means now the important place it was on the arrival of M. Berneux.

On the 31st of October 1840 he writes thus:

'Here we are at Macao at last, after eight months of travelling. A trial of patience indeed! but the thought of saving souls and of promoting the glory of God is the support of the missionary; and the pleasure of meeting with my brethren at Macao, and of at last arriving at my mission, makes up for all the fatigue and misery of the passage. O, if it be so blessed to arrive at an unknown place simply because God wills me to be there, what will not be the untold joy when, after years of pain and trouble, we shall arrive at our resting-place in heaven! Shall we regret any sacrifice made in order to attain so great a reward?.... Macao is my land of promise: with what joy have I not landed in this first town of the Celestial Empire, this soil which I shall not quit except to enter upon my mission! I can understand now how there may be circumstances so intensely happy, that in the midst of them one is inclined to exclaim, "It is enough!" Joy then becomes positive suffering, because the soul has not the capacity for receiving the torrents of sweetness with which it overflows. It was on the 21st of September, the Feast of St. Matthew, that we disembarked. We found Mgr. Retord at the missionary station, and three other missionaries, who are only waiting for the moment to set out. One, M. Taillandier, was a fellow-student of mine at Mans. I thank God for the consolation of this happy meeting, as, a fortnight later, he would not have been here. The destinations of some of us have been changed, in consequence of the continuance of the persecutions.

in Cochin-China and Tonquin. I know not where two of my *confrères* will be sent; but if the war ends, M. Maistre will probably go to Tonquin; and as for myself, it is almost certain that this will be my destination also. Our superiors tell us that if, notwithstanding the persecution, we are able to remain concealed there, I shall go with the Bishop on the first opportunity. I am delighted at this. I had feared to lose my destination—my dear Tonquin. I am working hard to know the language. We have Chinese, Cochin-Chinese, Tonquinese, and Corean pupils in the college. During my stay here I have the charge of educating two Coreans and one Tonquinese.'*

In another letter he writes of Macao:

'I do not yet know this place. Missionaries begin to be really missionaries here. They are obliged to conceal themselves, and to wear a disguise when they go out. The Chinese do not like us; still I am the happiest of men. Only pray for me, that God of His goodness may make me more holy, more detached from myself.'

After describing the costume of the Chinese—which he of course adopted on his arrival at Macao—together with the food and habits of the country, he concludes thus:

'Such are the ways which the missionary must adopt. He must make himself all to all, that he may gain all. If nature finds some difficulty in chang-

---

* The two Coreans were Andrew Kim and Francis Tschoey, of whom we shall hear more later on in this narrative.

ing the habits of a lifetime, grace helps a man to conquer them. God never abandons His priest, nor those who desire supremely to serve Him, and to do His holy will. We are often surprised at finding so little repugnance or difficulty about certain things which at first we shuddered to think of. But I have not had, I assure you, the least difficulty in accustoming myself to my new mode of life; indeed, were it necessary to suffer a thousand times more than I do, I would bear it with joy, were it but for the salvation of a single soul.'

It was during the stay of M. Berneux at Macao that the ship in which M. Taillandier sailed was seized by the satellites of the mandarin, four days after his departure from that place. 'At first,' so he writes to Mgr. Bouvier, 'some hope was entertained of a ransom; but the money we sent simply gratified the avarice of these men, without inducing them to release their victim.'

On the 21st of October he was put through his first interrogatory; but that he might not compromise the Chinese missions, nor the head-quarters at Macao, he refused to make any reply. One touching incident took place on the trial, showing at once the calm and generous spirit with which the souls of these devoted men accepted all the horrors of their position, and how strikingly they were supported by that grace which is sufficient for all our needs. The mandarin had ordered the missionary to be rudely struck; and being unable, even by this means, to induce him to speak, he endeavoured to force him to write. M. Taillandier took up his pen and wrote, '*Spiritus Domini, conforta me in bonum finem.*'

He was thrown into a prison with fifty criminals of the lowest sort, and exposed to every kind of suffering, both from cold and hunger. A Chinese gentleman who went to see him found him fastened to the ground in such a way that he could not move hand or foot, with no covering but a ragged old shirt, seated in the midst of every description of filth, and with a cold rain falling on his bare shoulders. He had been locked up in an inner dungeon, so that his visitor had to pass through eleven gates before arriving at his prison; but fortunately he was able, by bribing the jailor, to procure some straw and other alleviations for the martyr, who was suffering agonies from inflammation of the bowels, consequent on the sufferings he had undergone.

It was through the intervention of the English Admiral Elliot that M. Taillandier was at length released from the miseries of his captivity. He returned to Macao, to await a fresh appointment; and from thence in his turn was able to give accounts of Mgr. Berneux, when the latter was himself arrested.

At length the long-desired moment arrived, and M. Berneux was permitted to announce his approaching departure for the mission of Tonquin. Mgr. Retord writes thus:

'Our return will be perilous. Very possibly after having received the mitre, a blow may come which will deprive me at once of my mitre and my head. Nothing but miseries and distresses await me. I can see them looming in the distance, like dark smouldering volcanos; but, thanks be to God, I fear them not. I desire nothing but to finish my course and to do the work which our Lord has intrusted to me.'

To M. Nouart, M. Berneux in the fulness of his heart writes thus:

'The Chinese vessel has just arrived which is to convey me to Tonquin. Being taken at last by surprise, I am unable to make any satisfactory preparation. . . . In four days I shall leave with Monseigneur and a Spanish Dominican monk, and after about three days' sail we shall arrive at Annam. But in what state shall we find this unhappy country? Desolated, in all probability, by a fierce persecution. No news concerning it has been received for a whole twelvemonth. This silence is ominous. Then how shall we effect an entrance? The entire coast is guarded by twelve men-of-war, stationed by the king as a defence against the English. And being there, where shall we hide ourselves? What house will receive us? To none of these questions can we imagine even a reply, and I confess I do not trouble myself much to find one. It is enough that I am going there. If no house, no forest, no cave can be found to give me shelter, then will Minh-Mênh open to me his prisons; and, later on, God in His infinite mercy will, I trust, open to me the gates of heaven. I am happy, indeed, in having arrived at the end to which I have so long aspired. I am about to become a real missionary! Now I shall live, I hope, in the midst of privations of every description. Farewell, O ye pleasant walks of Allonnes and Couptrain! henceforth a hole dug in the ground will be my sole dwelling-place, and I shall not leave it except to fly from the mandarin. But if in this narrow spot I may never find the friend to whom I owe infinitely more than life itself (for what is life if not employed in the glory of God?), I shall surely always have Him who makes it His delight to dwell amongst the children of men.

'I was overjoyed when Mgr. Retord decided definitely upon taking me with him. Tonquin offers more means of sanctification to a priest than any other mission. His life there approaches more nearly to that of our Divine Lord in its many sources of suffering. Henceforth, indeed, I may call misery my spouse. We are to possess nothing of our own. All is to be placed in the hands of the Vicar-apostolic, who supplies each one according to his need. His living is poor. Rice and tea are his only food; a mat his bed: all his clothing consists in a pair of drawers and a tunic. Shirt, stockings, shoes—these are superfluities, and the missionary can forego them : true he may be cold, but our Lord Jesus Christ was cold also.

'And then even these meagre resources very often fail. For many years past, the ships containing the supplies for head-quarters have been exposed to robberies by pirates, and such losses are not easily repaired. Would you believe also, that in order to convey us three to Tonquin, it has been necessary to pay the captain 1400 piastres, or 8400 francs (356*l.*)?'

CHAPTER V.

Passage to Tonquin. Arrival. Death of Minh-Mênh. Missionaries separate. M. Berneux is left in hiding in a convent.

ON the 3d of January 1841 Mgr. Retord quitted Macao with three missionaries—MM. Galy and Berneux, and a Spanish Dominican, F. Emmanuel Rivas—together with six young Cochin-Chinese. They were twelve days in making a passage which a European vessel would have easily performed in two or three. It is not difficult to imagine the miseries to which the missionaries were exposed in so small a craft, obliged as they were to keep themselves always concealed, and a prey therefore to all kinds of vermin. They landed on the 16th of January; and Mgr. Retord, after having located MM. Berneux and Galy in a Christian village, was fortunate enough to regain his own straw hut, which he called his episcopal palace. He arrived there at one o'clock on the morning of the 20th January, the day and the hour upon which the tyrant Minh-Mênh expired.

Mgr. Retord writes:

'After a reign of terror, whereby this cruel prince had at last reduced his people to a kind of frightened silence and submission, and just as he was promising himself a long life, a fall from his horse ruptured his bowels; and after horrible tortures, which no doctors could relieve, he died in agony; while the religion which he flattered himself he had utterly annihilated is still flourishing and fruitful, and as much consoled by fresh conquests as she is proud of her numberless martyrs.'

In a letter dated 22d January Mgr. Berneux gives the following details of the arrival of the missionaries at Tonquin:

'On the 11th of this month we sighted the mountains of Eastern Tonquin. This view gave me inexpressible joy. The Annamites, on the contrary, appeared melancholy at the sight of their own country, which rejects both them and their religion. Monseigneur also appeared a little depressed; not, indeed, for himself, but for his mission and for us. He was afraid that he might only have brought us from Macao to throw us into the hands of the mandarins.

'For two days we were detained in one spot by a dead calm. Had it not been for this *contretemps*, we should have been taken prisoners just as we landed. It appears that about forty Chinese barques having arrived on the coast for the purpose of fishing, the mandarins, who can think of nothing but of English ships, mistook them for European vessels. . . . At once a multitude of armed men came down upon the coast to oppose the expected invasion. After two days the Chinese barques retired, and the mandarins decamped, no doubt in a state of great felicity at having intimidated the English fleet.

'On the 15th, about two o'clock in the afternoon,

a little ship, manned by Christians, came to take us ashore. We wished to wait till nightfall; but the Chinese drove us from their vessel, under pretence that they expected a domiciliary visit from the mandarins. In this way we were very nearly shipwrecked, for the sea was rough, and our boat very small... After all, there is nothing to surprise one in such conduct: they were but pagans; but what a change comes over the heart of man when religion has once taken possession of it! Amongst the heathen we found nothing but egotism, and an entire absence of all higher feelings; but as for all the Christians whom I have met since I came here, their devotion is perfectly heroic.

'After sailing all day on the 16th, we approached the shore of Western Tonquin. There we were transferred into the boat of some other fishermen; and on the morning of the 17th, after wandering for a long time in the open country, we arrived at last amongst our neophytes, at a village called Phat-Diem, in the province of Ninh-Binh. For three nights we had not closed our eyes; we were too glad, therefore—the Bishop, M. Galy, and I—to rest for a few hours upon the same bed.

'The priest of this little place, an old man of seventy years, had just been seized as he was leaving his hiding-place in order to go to confession; we were therefore unable to remain long in a village exposed to fresh visitations of this kind; and the same evening we continued our journey. Clothed in a tunic and trousers reaching to the knee, with hats made of leaves about six feet in size, we rather resembled brigands who are about to set fire to and pillage some unfortunate village, than missionaries about to conquer souls. For four hours we walked through very rugged paths. My feet, which are not as yet accustomed to do without shoes, did not relish much this fashion of the country. Still, notwithstanding the pain I felt when I happened to cut them upon a soil which the sun had baked, and which was often as sharp as little flints, I could not help laughing at thinking of the appearance we presented. The night was dark, and we seldom could see the spot where we placed our feet; and sometimes, in raising one's foot to avoid a stone or a mound of earth, we fell flat into a hole.

'At one o'clock in the morning we found ourselves in the parish of Phuc-Nhac. Here M. Galy will remain until some vessel arrives which can take him on to join M. Masson. Monseigneur is stationed about four or five leagues from hence, with M. Charrier; and as for myself, I am in hiding in a convent at Yen-Moi. I believe Monseigneur intends to send me also eventually to join M. Masson, where things are rather more quiet; but I cannot tell whether events will be sufficiently favourable to permit this. In the mean while I intend to study hard the Annamite language, that I may the sooner make myself useful. I shall have plenty of time; no one but the people of the house know of my retreat; I receive no visits but only those of the good Master, who day by day before sunrise comes to strengthen me, and to sweeten with His presence my little mud cabin. And here, though I can but take six steps in it; though I can only speak under my breath, and see no daylight except through a crevice in the wall made a few inches above ground ; and, to crown all, although in order to read or write I am obliged to lie my whole length upon my mat, I consider myself as the happiest of men.'

These details are completed in a letter to his mother. He says : 'Our entrance into Tonquin has been somewhat fatiguing; but now I lead a very quiet life: it is amongst some nuns that I have found a refuge. Do not fancy, however, that these convents in any way resemble those at home. Imagine a number of little mud cabins, roofed with straw, in which about twenty poor girls have established themselves, anxious for the salvation of their souls, and supporting themselves by incessant labour. Such is a Tonquin convent: my room is one of these cabins ; my furniture consists of a mat, spread upon three boards, raised about a foot from the ground. This is my bed, my armchair, and my writing-table. The room is lighted by a little hole in the wall, about a foot square, nearly on a level with the ground; so that for me the sun rises about nine o'clock, and sets at three in the afternoon. A small plate filled with black oil gives me a little light from six o'clock to eight. Then it is necessary to extinguish it on account of the thieves, who are numerous enough in these parts. Monseigneur has given me two young persons to wait upon me. One, my "minister of the interior," has the care of my table; the other, my "minister of foreign affairs," keeps watch outside. Would you like to have an idea of an Annamite dinner? Upon a little round table without legs, about six inches high, are placed three or four little plates filled with fish and pork, vegetables and oranges. I eat with two little sticks, like a Chinaman, squatted on my mat. . . . . There is a kind of wine made from rice, but I do not like it. I prefer tea without sugar or milk, which is the beverage of the country. There is no bread of any kind. . . . . . . Melancholy as this description must appear to you, I assure you I have never been happier in my life. Without fear or anxiety of any sort I leave myself with perfect confidence in the hands of God. I occupy myself without ceasing in the study of the language, that I may lose no time in working for the glory of God and the salvation of souls. I have omitted to mention the altar in my room; yet here it is that I find all my happiness. A single Mass amply repays the little sacrifices I have to make. I only wish, dear mother, I could make you taste the happiness I experience, when, assisted by my catechist, and surrounded by the nuns of this poor convent, I pray for you, for my family, for my country, and for this kingdom, which is in such great need of prayers. O, then, indeed, you would not pity me!"

CHAPTER VI.

Tonquin. Brief summary of its geographical position, and the history of the Church during the 240 years of its existence. Hopes entertained at the commencement of the present century. Successful negotiations on the part of the Vicar-apostolic of Cochin-China with the King of France to restore Gia Laong to the throne. Ingratitude of this monarch. His death, and the cruel reign of his son Minh-Mênh.

TONQUIN, or that portion of the Annamite empire which M. Berneux had reached with so much toil and danger, is divided into twelve provinces, covering an area of 30,000 square kilometres. Its population is reckoned at 15,000,000; which, according to its comparative extent, is three times greater than that of France.

It was in the year 1626 that the faith was first preached in these countries by Father Baldinotti, an Italian Jesuit, assisted by the Fathers Marquès and de Rhodes. Their labours were crowned with the most unparalleled success; for only three years after the commencement of their mission, this infant Church reckoned 82,000 neophytes. Persecution did not retard the work or shake the faith of the new Christians, although again and again the missionaries were driven from their flocks. It was during one of these temporary exiles that Father de Rhodes visited Paris, where he assisted in the foundation of the 'Séminaire des Missions Etrangères,' which has since given so many apostles and martyrs to the Church.

On their return, the good missionaries not only had the great joy of witnessing the perseverance of their beloved disciples, but of finding also large numbers of fresh converts added to the flock. In the years 1645 and 1646 alone, 22,000 heathens renounced their idols; and in 1679, thirty-three years later, Pope Innocent XI. consolidated this most interesting mission by dividing it into two separate vicariates, and appointing Mgr. Pallu, Bishop of Heliopolis, and Mgr. de Bourges, Bishop of Auren, as its first Vicars-apostolic.

During the seventeenth century the persecution only ceased at rare intervals; but it was in the eighteenth that it began to be the most cruel. Then it was that men were called upon to shed their blood for the faith; and the country being moreover a prey to civil wars, the Christians were among the first to suffer.

At the beginning of the present century the conquest of Tonquin by the King of Cochin-China appeared likely to pave the way for a time of peace for the Church. The king, Gia Laong, having been driven from his throne by his rebellious subjects, had recourse to Mgr. Pigneaux de Béhaine, the Bishop of Adran and Vicar-apostolic of Cochin-China. This prelate undertook his cause, and in fact concluded a treaty for him with the King of France.

On his return from Europe, Mgr. Béhaine procured from the governor of the French Indies three armed men-of-war, together with French officers, who organised the Cochin-Chinese army and fleet, assisted the king in a complete triumph over the rebels, and, farther, procured for him the conquest of Tonquin, the sovereign of which had frequently abetted the disaffected subjects of Gia Laong and invaded Cochin-China.

Unhappily, Mgr. de Béhaine was carried off in the fifty-ninth year of his age, just as he might fairly hope to reap the fruit of his political labours for the salvation of souls and the glory of our Lord Jesus Christ. The king caused his funeral to be performed with truly royal magnificence, and raised a tomb to his memory, which still exists, and which, situated on a territory which has since fallen under French rule, has become a monument which will certainly perpetuate the remembrance of the gratitude of the king, and the services rendered to his country by the illustrious bishop.

Two years after the death of Mgr. Pigneaux, his royal pupil, Prince Canh, whom the holy bishop had adopted during his exile, and brought up in the faith, followed him at the age of twenty-three years. Thus vanished prematurely the greatest hope of the Annamite mission; for the double tie which united Christianity to the sovereign power being now broken, Gia Laong considered himself free to be ungrateful. Together with his benefactor and his child, he lost the remembrance of past services, and broke all the promises he had made in days of adversity of protection to the Christians. But although he replied to their appeals by menaces, the persecution was as yet delayed; and the missionaries took advantage of his toleration to carry the faith into every corner of his kingdom; so though this reign did not accomplish all it appeared to promise, it was nevertheless one of the most fruitful for the Christian Apostolate, as it was the most glorious for the Annamite empire.

In 1820 Minh-Mênh, son of a concubine, succeeded Gia Laong, to the detriment of the son of Prince Canh. It is said that on his death-bed Gia Laong, terrified by the sanguinary projects of his son, exhorted him to continue the same ambiguous policy with regard to the Christians that he had begun. But of what avail were exhortations such as these to a prince who prided himself upon having taken for his model the most cruel tyrant of Japan, solely because he had exterminated all the neophytes in his dominions, and fully earned the title of the Annamite Nero, by the infernal rage he employed, during the twenty years of his reign, for the extermination of the Christian faith?

In February 1825 Minh-Mênh published an edict forbidding the entrance of any European, and more particularly of any missionary, into his territories. Under one pretext or another he contrived to possess himself of the persons of several of the principal missionaries; the rest took refuge in concealment.

According to the instructions of the Holy See, the missionaries had devoted a large portion of their labours to the formation of a native clergy. Two seminaries had been founded for this purpose at Tonquin, each of which numbered about forty students. In 1823 nineteen Annamite priests were ordained, raising the number of native priests to ninety-three. This was a most necessary provision against the approaching persecution. At such times it is much more easy for native priests than for Europeans to conceal themselves, or to move about for the administration of the Sacraments; while the presence alone of the European missionary gives encouragement to both clergy and laity.

Every preparation was now made before the publication of the edict. The pupils of the seminaries were dispersed in different districts, where they might in safety continue their studies. Everywhere the wooden churches were taken to pieces, in order to avoid profanation, and the materials hidden, whilst awaiting happier times.

At length, in 1830, the edict appeared which exposed the Christians to apostacy or death, and this persecution continued without intermission until the death of the tyrant. In an oration pronounced in the secret consistory of the 27th of April 1840, Pope Gregory XVI. compared the glorious triumphs of the martyrs of Cochin-China and Tonquin to those of the Christians of the first ages. Not only have we to record the martyrdoms of the two Vicars-apostolic of Eastern Tonquin, Mgrs. Ignace Delgado and Dominic Henarès, Mgr. Borie-Dumoulin, Bishop-elect, and the Fathers Jean Charles Cornay, François Jaccard, Marchand, Gagelin, Joseph Henarès, and Odorico; but also of nine native priests and five catechists, with a crowd of native Christians, who bore the martyr's glorious palm, and confessed the faith of Jesus Christ in the midst of the most frightful torments. Such is the power of faith, and one of its greatest miracles, that it can inspire heroism even in a people who are accustomed to tremble before the will of those who govern them.

It was this afflicted Church, so glorious to the eye of faith, which Mgr. Retord, Bishop of Acanthe, was called upon to govern, and for whose sake M. Berneux was now about to enter into the bloody arena of martyrdom.

CHAPTER VII.

Discovery of MM. Galy and Berneux. They are taken prisoners, and put in cages. Conduct of neophytes and Christians. Imprisonment at Nam-Dinh. Examinations. Departure for and journey to Hué. Arrival.

THE village of Phuc-Nhac had been chosen for the present retreat of MM. Galy and Berneux, its neighbourhood to the sea affording facilities for their intended journey to the province of Xu-Nghê. They were on the point of starting, and the ship which was to convey them was already prepared, when, on the morning of Easter day, immediately after the celebration of holy Mass, their little dwelling was surrounded by five hundred soldiers, headed by the grand mandarin Nam-Dinh. By order of the late king, this latter had set all his spies to work, in order to find the Dominican F. Hermozilla, and by this means had fallen in with the retreat of MM. Galy and Berneux. Flight was impossible. They fell at once, with nineteen Christians, into the hands of the mandarin.

In a letter written from prison on the 25th of August 1841, M. Berneux gives the following details of his arrest, his interrogatories, and his imprisonment. We insert this letter at full length, since it is one of the most glorious MSS. which we possess of our holy confessor:

Since you desire to learn all, even the most trifling details of our history, I will try and satisfy you. I had passed Holy Week in meditation on the sufferings of our Lord: on the Saturday evening, having received fresh orders from Mgr. the Vicar-apostolic, I rejoiced in the thought that I should soon be sent near you. That same evening I heard some confessions — the first-fruits of my ministry on the Annamite territory, and also the last: the designs of God are unsearchable, but always to be adored.

The following morning, being that of the Resurrection, I administered the Bread of Heaven to the little flock which surrounded me: precious victims, indeed, whom I thus adorned for sacrifice; valiant athletes, whom I thus armed for the combat, and, I trust, also for victory. I had not yet put off my sacred vestments, when close to me I heard the crier of the mandarin. He commanded the men of the village to assemble together in a certain spot, in order that the soldiers might search their dwellings with greater ease. I had already once been obliged to fly from the honour of a visit from the mandarin, but this time retreat was impossible. I left the retreat which had been my hospitable home for two months, and took refuge amongst the nuns. This dwelling was not calculated for a place of concealment. I was reduced to the necessity of installing myself upon some bamboos suspended from the wall;

and there, seated in a basket of onions, I awaited the soldiers in perfect security, adoring Him whom I had just received for the last time.

Very shortly after, about a dozen satellites invaded my dwelling. For a long time I heard them with their pikes and their guns promenading beneath my hiding-place, asking questions of the only nun who was left in the house. She replied in few words, then turned from them and wept. At the same time, in order to conceal me more effectually, she set fire to some straw underneath my perch, and thus enveloped me in a thick cloud of smoke: in the excess of her zeal or of her fear, she happened to warm me a little more than was actually convenient. Twice the pikes of these inquisitors raised the trellis upon which I was lying, without discovering my presence. At last some soldiers, more clear-sighted than the rest, drew me from the asylum where I was really far from comfortable. They seized me with a cry of unexpected joy, and after relieving me of everything which suited their fancy, conducted me into the presence of the mandarin.

It was with a feeling of intense joy that I found myself dragged by these soldiers, in the same manner that our adorable Saviour was dragged from the garden of Olives to Jerusalem. Their chief took from me my scapular, my rosary, and the reliquary hanging round my neck. As I was covered with sweat and with soot, they gave me water to wash myself, and then tied my hands behind my back. Soon after, my companion M. Galy arrived. 'This is indeed a happy day!' he exclaimed, as he embraced me. 'Yes,' I replied, 'this is the day truly that the Lord has made; let us rejoice and be glad.'

It appeared that M. Galy was preparing to say Mass when he learned the news of the approach of the mandarin. He was sent away directly from the house which had harboured him, and was completely abandoned. Repulsed from every hut where he endeavoured to find a retreat, tracked like a wild beast, he at length threw himself into a ditch under some bamboos. Here the soldiers passed him without seeing him, and he was able to recite his office and to sleep. He was at length discovered; but although he was roughly handled in his capture, and in taking his reliquary they had to break the double cord which attached it to his neck, he felt no pain, but rejoined me, reciting the Te Deum. Soon after, under the guard of the soldiers, arrived seven native Christians, mostly catechists, with three women, two of whom were nuns. I recognised one of the latter; I made a sign to her, pointing to the sky, that she should put her trust in God. She replied by a smile, as though to explain how well she appreciated the grace with which she had been favoured by our Lord.

It might now be about two o'clock in the afternoon. M. Galy and I were forbidden to communicate with each other; nevertheless my dearly-beloved companion was able to confess whilst we took our repast. We agreed also to feign a total ignorance of the Annamite language, which, having so lately entered the country, was no difficult matter. A jailer inquired our name. According to the resolution we had taken, we allowed him for half an hour to exhaust himself in efforts to make us comprehend these little words, 'Ten la gi,' What is your name? At length, taking pity on the poor scribe, we informed him that in Europe we were called Galy and Berneux; but being necessary to write these names in Chinese characters, every one endeavoured to reproduce in the idiom of the country the sounds I had just articulated; and the scene became really curious.

After severely scourging many of the inhabitants of the village, and night having set in, the Christians arrested with us were loaded with the *cangue*, whilst my confrère and myself were placed in a cage, in which my long legs found scarcely sufficient room to bestow themselves. Being arrived on the banks of the river leading to the chief town of the province, I felt for a moment great sadness of heart. M. Galy appeared about to continue his journey by land, whilst I was to be taken in a boat: perhaps we were thus to be separated for ever; but I submitted myself to the will of God, and my spirit was restored to its usual calm. Although resigned, I was joyful enough the following morning to find that I had been mistaken, and that my confrère was in another bark, behind me.

That day a Christian neophyte sent me the simple repast he had prepared for me: my soldiers, considering doubtless that it was not worthy of me, adjudged it to themselves. Thus I went without breakfast, and it was the same with dinner.

When we arrived at Nam-Dinh it was nearly

nightfall. The whole population turned out to witness our landing. I heard round my cage the crowd repeating with satisfaction: 'It is Father Vong—what a good prize!' Next they transferred the honour of the episcopate to M. Galy, when it was known that I was only twenty-seven years of age. We thought it better not to contradict this error, as it might put a stop to the search after Mgr. Hermozilla. From the people it passed to the mandarins, who have been confirmed in their opinion, partly by our silence, and partly by the misleading reports of many Cochin-Chinese.

We had now larger cages assigned us, though not till they had taken the precaution of chaining us. Our irons may possibly weigh from ten to twelve pounds. We wear them without as much fatigue as might be expected, except when we cannot sleep. The mandarin was much amused to see us help the workman employed in riveting the great rings on our feet. I could not help affectionately kissing this chain, which has become the source of our greatest confidence in the mercy of God. I offer it every day, for the expiation of my sins, to Him who upon Calvary bore a heavier instrument of torture for the salvation of the world.

Two Europeans being a sight sufficiently curious in this kingdom, permission was granted to open the prison-doors to whomsoever might desire to see us near. From morning till evening we were consequently besieged by numberless visitors; and the Christians were not the last to make their appearance. It was, indeed, with difficulty I could moderate their tokens of compassion, and decline their offers of charity, while pious mothers brought their little ones to receive my blessing. As for the heathen, some asked for medicines; others begged me to observe their features, or the lines in their hands, in order to foretell their future.

It became at last impossible for me to keep silence any longer. Having been unable to preach Jesus Christ when I was free, I tried to do so in my prison, for the benefit of our neophytes, and also to undeceive these poor idolaters, who know nothing of the Gospel except through the calumnies of its enemies. By means of the few Annamite words I had learned, I endeavoured to explain to the pagans the reason why we showed so much joy in our captivity.

'Here,' they exclaimed, 'it is usual to see chains worn with a melancholy face, whilst you appear happy.'

'Yes, because the Christian possesses a secret which you do not know. We are come to teach you how to be always happy, because we love you; but you, instead of profiting by it, seek to kill those who bring you this inestimable blessing.'

For about eight days these interviews continued, when, for some motive unknown to me, all access to my cage was forbidden, and I became the object of the most careful surveillance. I was continually surrounded by a numerous guard. Nevertheless I was able to hear the confessions of some Christians, who managed to reach me by means of bribes.

However, although my treatment was severe,

the mandarins of Nam-Dinh (I must say, to their credit) did all that lay in their power to make me forget the rigour of my captivity. They frequently visited me, and took pleasure in asking me questions upon the nature of Christianity. One day my guard asked me why, in our religion, priests were forbidden to marry. I answered, that it was part of the discipline of the Church; that if the priest had a family, he would live for *them*, he would strive to amass a fortune for their sakes, and would thus neglect the poor; whereas, relinquishing all home ties, all the world were his children, especially those who were poor and miserable; and if any were dying of hunger, they would find in the priest one who would share his last crust or his last bowl of rice with them.

This man repeated my answer to the mandarins, and one of them, pointing to a little boy, said to me:

'There is one of your children.'

'Yes,' I replied; 'but the child of sorrow.'

'Why?'

'Because I cannot feed him with the Bread of Life, or with the truth, which is the life of man. His own father opposes it.'

'No; I assure you I do not wish to prevent his listening to you or following your instructions.'

'Mandarin,' I replied, 'you know you do not speak seriously. If I were really to begin to teach your child, he would no longer be allowed to play near the bars of my cage.'

I also made friends with our guards. They shared with me their tea and betel, and acted in the same friendly manner towards M. Galy, who enjoyed more liberty, and was not condemned, as I was, to solitary confinement. He, on the contrary, was frequently visited by Christians; besides which, a whole family, who were prisoners for the faith, shared in his captivity. Three children, who had followed their parents to their prison, were in the habit of waiting upon him, and took the opportunity of giving him the customary salutation during the sleep of the soldiers. One of them said one day:

'The father suffers for Jesus Christ; but God assists and strengthens him.'

It is time now to speak of our interrogatories. M. Galy, being mistaken for Mgr. Hermozilla, was fortunately able without difficulty to evade the questions put to him. I myself was less fortunate.

[Then follows an account of the cross-questioning, from which but little information was gained by their examiners. At last, their patience being exhausted, they had recourse to cruel threats.]

'Have you no pity,' said a mandarin, 'upon that white-haired priest standing near your cage?'

'Yes, mandarin.'

'Would you be willing to bear his chains for him?'

'Most willingly. I am stronger than he is; and I would do it with yet greater pleasure if it could procure your conversion.'

'And I,' said the old man, 'would not part with this chain; it is my treasure.'

The mandarin: 'If you will not reply, those Annamite priests shall be beaten with rods.'

'I consider it useless to remind a judge of the laws of justice. If any one should suffer through my silence, it should be myself alone.'

Upon this the mandarins retired, and I took the opportunity to ask pardon of the aged priest for any ill-treatment which might befall him on my account. He begged me to be without disquiet.

On the following cross-examination a third judge was added to the two previous ones. One, whom I shall call *my friend,* on account of the urbanity with which he treated me during my captivity, asked me:

'Are you still happy?'

'I am.'

'Can you eat the food with which the mandarins furnish you at their own cost?'

'Yes; and I thank the mandarins for it.'

'Do you know Thang Sanh?' (This was the name adopted recently by one of M. Galy's clerks.)

'No, mandarin.'

Then they brought him forward, and removed a portion of his clothing, that I might see the marks of the rotin upon his body. It was a frightful sight. Then the rods were brought, and the mandarin questioned me again upon the place of my embarkation, the period of my arrival in Cochin-China, and the names of our catechists. Seeing that I did not reply to any of these questions, he said,

'Speak, or you will be beaten.'

'I am in your hands, mandarin; if you choose to beat me, you have the power; but I am not free to answer your questions.'

I was nevertheless not displeased to find that

they did not take me at my word; yet I believe I could have borne it better than the apparent indifference I was forced to assume on beholding the grievous torments which those devoted men had endured on our account. But they understood it; for only in this way could I avoid compromising them still farther.

In another and final examination, after having drawn up the indictment, the friendly mandarin said to me:

'Are you very anxious that this religion should be established in Cochin-China?'

'Very, mandarin. It is for this very purpose that I am come, at the peril of my life.'

'Hold! Here are men about to die,' added he, pointing out our three Annamite clerics. 'Advise them to abjure your religion for one month only; they can then resume it, and their lives will be saved.'

'Mandarin, no one can advise a father to sacrifice his own children. Yet you would ask a priest to counsel his Christians to apostatise!' Then turning to the three confessors, I said to them, 'I have but one advice to give to you: think that you are approaching the end of all your sufferings, whilst the happiness which awaits you is eternal. Merit it by constancy.'

They promised.

[The mandarin then questioned M. Berneux on that future life of which he spoke.]

'Where,' said he, laughing, 'does the soul go on its departure from the body?'

I answered his inquiry, and added, 'You laugh, mandarin; the time will come when you will laugh no longer.' . . .

My friend the mandarin sought me after some days, accompanied by the three confessors of whom I have spoken. He showed me a paper written by my catechist, representing that I had been nine years in Tonquin; that I had been taken with a Spaniard, a friend of mine, named Trùm Vong. He besought me to conform my replies in future to this declaration. It was a great grief to me thus constantly to refuse the requests of men who had really shown me great good-will; but I was obliged to do so. I told him that I would do all I could to shield my first interlocutors, but that I could not confirm these declarations, which were altogether false. But I hoped to be able to compromise no one.

Shortly before our departure, the same mandarin brought my catechist, that I might have the pleasure of seeing him for the last time. I announced to him that I was about to be sent to the royal city, where I knew that nothing but torments awaited me; and again I exhorted him to constancy. He replied, 'We shall esteem ourselves happy in following our two fathers, and in dying with them.'

Then came a fresh interrogatory both of M. Galy and myself. . . . . It was remarkable how, in the case of M. Galy, the guards themselves were proud of his courage, and carried him back to his prison in a kind of triumph. I was unable myself to remain until the conclusion of this cross-examination, for the judge, perceiving that I was suffering from fever, gave orders that I should be reconducted to prison..... [They again besought him to answer in the sense suggested, which he refused.]

It was on the 9th of May that we left this place, each of us carried by twelve Annamites. From one hundred and fifty to two hundred soldiers, armed with pikes and ranged in double file, formed our escort. In the midst of the detachment our cages were carried, and surrounding us were four or five mandarins, who accompanied us as far as the gates of the town. Our good neophytes did not fail to meet us on the road. I was delighted to see once more the little ones who had visited me in prison, and who hid themselves behind the soldiers in order to make me their three salutations. I replied by a smile, then covering their faces with their hands, they turned away and wept.

Our march was excessively painful, especially during the passage across Tonquin. The royal road in this part of the kingdom is not to be compared with the very worst road in France, intersected as it is continually by ravines and brooks, which are crossed by broken bridges. The difficulties were greater still during the passage of the mountains separating Tonquin from Cochin-China. Although our cages were each borne by twenty men, it was with great difficulty that we reached the summit; but in descending the opposite side, so rapid was the declivity, that it was necessary to slide them, by means of cords, along the edges of rocks and precipices. Thus we journeyed for nineteen days, starting by torchlight about one or two hours before daybreak, and halting for some time at midday, after which we resumed our journey till night. But great as were our sufferings, the fatigues of our journey were constantly compensated, either by the beauty of the scenery, or the anxiety of the Christians to see and do honour to their spiritual fathers thus imprisoned for the faith. You would scarcely believe with what touching obstinacy they would cling to the bars of our cages, and rend the air with their cries, as we moved away from them. In the first province of Cochin-China they ran in crowds before the cortège. The soldiers could not proceed, and the mandarins themselves were obliged to order our cages to be set down on the ground, in order that these unhappy neophytes might have time to express their grief and their veneration. Even the pagans joined the Christians in offering us fruit and money; but these we always declined, telling them that we needed nothing of them but their prayers. When it was absolutely necessary to resume our march, the Christians were so earnest in their solicitations to be allowed to carry us, that the soldiers were compelled to resign their burden as far as the river. Here neither the rotin nor the menaces of the soldiers prevented them from following us as far as they could, and even on the opposite shore we could hear their sobs distinctly.

I then found out that during this time our mandarins had been in a perfect agony. 'Do you know,' they exclaimed, 'that those people wanted to rescue you?' 'Well,' I replied, 'it would have been easy enough. But we should ourselves have objected.'

'Why ?' 'Because it would have cost you your lives; and I do not think you would give them up as readily as we should.'

I was immensely touched at all we had seen and heard. My whole soul was wrung at the thought of that devoted flock dispersed as sheep without a shepherd, or any one to break to them the Bread of Life. I could only conjure our merciful Saviour to bring the misfortunes of these poor people to an end, and grant them at last the blessing of peace.

In every chief town in the province we received the visit of the mandarins, who showed us as much consideration as lay in their power. One in particular, an old man, congratulated us on our serenity, and begged us to lose none of our resignation; after which he made the sign of the cross. 'Mandarin,' I replied, 'it is not sufficient to make the external sign—you ought to know and practise our holy religion. If the king and his officers knew it, they would cease this persecution.'

At length, on the 28th of May, we arrived at the capital. As we approached, I felt as though a slight cloud passed over my soul: were we not entering the tiger's den? But it lasted only a little while; and when the walls of Hué became visible, my joy and confidence were redoubled.

CHAPTER VIII.

Examinations at Hué. Missionaries commanded to dishonour the Cross. They refuse, and are put to the torture. They are insulted both in their prisons and in the streets. They are found guilty of preaching the Gospel, and condemned to death.

WE had feared, in consequence of our examinations at Nam-Dinh, that we should be judged as rebels, and not as missionaries; but it pleased God at once, on our arrival, to dissipate this fear; for hardly were we presented to the grand mandarin than we were commanded to trample the Cross under foot.

M. Galy was first interrogated.

'How long have you been in Tonquin?'

'I left Cadiz four years ago.'

'If these chains were removed, would you continue to preach?'

'If I could,' he exclaimed, 'I would preach to the death.'

The mandarin then addressed similar questions to me; after which, seizing upon a Cross, he ordered my companion to trample upon it.

'No,' cried he, 'let me die rather!'

I took the Cross in order to kiss it; as I was prevented doing this, I turned to the judges, saying:

'If it be a question of life or death, I am ready

to offer my head to the executioner; but command me to apostatise, and I must resist to the last.'

By order of the mandarin, a soldier trampled upon the Cross before our eyes.

'Is that action a crime?' said he.

I did not reply.

'He is angry,' said the mandarin.

'No, indeed,' I said; 'but I am grieved at this profanation.'

'Is it wicked to tread upon the Cross?'

'This crucifix,' I replied, 'is the image of God; if it were proposed to you to insult your father's image, would you do it? Now God is the Father of all; He loves us as His children; to tread under foot His image is a fearful crime. I would sooner die than be guilty of it.'

'And who is God?' continued the mandarin.

'He is the Eternal Being, who has created heaven and earth. His power is boundless; in His hands is life and death.'

'If He has infinite power, why does He not destroy the profaners of His Cross?'

'Because He is good; and desires to give His children time to repent and amend.'

'Why does He not deliver you from your chains?'

'He sometimes permits the wicked to triumph in this world; but in the next they will be punished, and the just will be recompensed.'

'Do men, then, live again after death?'

'Yes; and he who has done good will enter into eternal happiness; he who has done evil will endure an eternity of misery.' (The mandarin smiled.) 'You smile: the time is not far distant when you will know which of us is right.'

Once more we were urged to trample upon the Cross: on our refusal, our first examination came to an end.

We were examined four times before being put to the torture.

During the last examination these were the concluding questions:

'What does your religion teach?'

'To flee from vice, and to practise virtue.'

'Practise virtue!' exclaimed the mandarin wrathfully; and passing quickly to another subject, 'You lie,' said he, 'when you pretend ignorance of the names that I desire to know.'

'Did we wish to deceive, what would be more easy? I could say, I have spent part of my time in this city; I have been received and hidden in your house, mandarin.'

Upon this the mandarin made a horrible grimace, whilst the interpreter begged me not to bring the judge into question, otherwise I should be beaten. Being once more desired to give up the names of the Annamites whom I might know, I again refused. My hands were then tied, as the demand was reiterated. A soldier brought the Cross, whilst two others seized me in order to drag me across the instrument of our salvation. I resisted, crying out, 'I will not, I will not!' M. Galy, who was not in the circle, threw himself towards me, exclaiming, 'We will not!' Then taking up the

Cross and kissing it, he exclaimed, 'Rather die a thousand times than profane it!'

Then I was stretched upon the ground, and after having pinioned my hands and feet, the mandarin continued:

'Tell the truth, or you shall be beaten to death.'

'I have already spoken the truth,' was my reply. 'Strike, if you choose.'

For some time I was kept in this position; but heavy rain came on, and we were sent back to prison.

On the 13th of June they did not confine themselves to menaces; after the interrogatory followed the bastinado. M. Galy received twenty lashes of the rotin, myself but seven. We had prayed for grace to suffer with becoming dignity, without uttering a cry. This prayer was granted; a stone could not have been more silent, more immovable. The blows followed each other slowly, and between each M. Galy was asked whether he suffered.

'Much,' he replied.

'See,' exclaimed a mandarin, 'the soldier is tired of striking, but he is not of suffering!'

The following morning the same torture; I received thirteen lashes over the wounds of the previous day. When I raised my head in order to reply to my judges, I heard them say:

'His face is not changed; it is as though they merely struck the ground.'

After me, M. Galy received ten more blows. The rotin is a horrible thing. Each time it fell upon our bodies it left a bloody ridge from five to six inches long. *Danh dan!* (Strike hard!) cried the mandarin to the executioner; and he, on his part, did his work conscientiously. One might have taken his stick for a rod of red-hot iron. Soon may come the tenter-hooks and nails; they shall be welcome! The grace of God, which sustains us, will be stronger than their tortures. May Jesus live for evermore!

During the first days of our sojourn in the royal city the people pressed upon us from all parts; not, as in the provinces, to testify sympathy and respect, but in order to pursue us with curses and blasphemy: from the aged man to the little child, every one made a point of injuring us, and of giving us a blow with his stick. Not even the enclosure of the prison was any protection from the popular hate. More than once, when, during the evening, we sought a little pure air in the courtyard, we have been obliged to reënter the doors in order to escape the showers of stones which were thrown at us. How, indeed, can it be otherwise, with the absurd stories which calumny has taken care to spread on our behalf! In the eyes of these poor idolaters we are considered as mysterious malevolent beings, ready to employ some supernatural power in our possession against them. Would you believe that I was seriously asked, whilst under the blows of the executioner, whether it was not true that I had taken the eyes of a little child in order to make holy water? Poor creatures!

I have omitted to mention that our road from the prison to the tribunal was strewn with crosses. Blessed be our dear Saviour, who not only associates us with His humiliations, but even permits that they should make use of us in order to insult Him! In return, we will glorify Him as much as we can by our sufferings.

* * * * * *

My beloved brethren, the hour of my liberty has expired. I hasten to seal up this letter. All that my heart can contain of respect, gratitude, and devotion is yours. By the contents of this long epistle you will see the power of grace, for which I entreat you to praise and magnify the God of mercy, who has thus vouchsafed to shower His favours on one so unworthy of the least of these His gifts. May He deign to bless your mission! May He cause brighter days to dawn upon you and upon this unhappy people! Such is my hourly prayer.

Pray for me now and after my death, which I do not believe to be so near as you think. I have written two words to my mother, which I beg Mgr. Cuenot to forward to Europe. . . .

Farewell, my dear friends; farewell in this world, this place of exile, of trouble, of sin. In heaven there will be true peace. Pray that I may soon be there, to offer up for you prayers that our Lord is willing to grant. I embrace you *in osculo sancto*.

BERNEUX.

'This letter may be considered as perfectly free from exaggeration.   GALY.'

P.S. You have commanded me to report without omission our examinations and our sufferings, from the beginning of our captivity up to the present day. I have obeyed, from a principle of duty and gratitude. Now, my dear sirs and brothers in Jesus Christ, there remains but one request which I would make. Let not this communication pass into other hands; do not make use of it, except to correct the exaggerated reports which may get abroad. Let it simply be known that we have compromised no one, and that our good Master overwhelms us with His graces. Let this silence be a pledge of your friendship for me. I ask it in consideration of my chain, which you reverence. I ask it for the glory of God, to whom appertains the honour of taking the humble reed, and of exposing it to the fury of the winds, while He hinders it from being broken by the tempest, in order to show forth the strength of His almighty arm.

In life, in death, and after death,

BERNEUX.

Feeling assured that death could not be long delayed, Mgr. Berneux wrote a few pencil-lines to his mother, with an injunction not to forward them to her until his martyrdom was accomplished.

'My dearest mother,—God has deigned to crown the favours He has granted me through life by the supreme honour of suffering for His Name's sake. The fear of being surprised by my gaolers compels me to write only these few words. I am happy; happier than ever. O, how sweet it is to suffer for our good God! Love Him, dearest mother. Love

Him, my good little sister. Love Him, my dear Frederick; for He is infinitely to be loved. I beseech this of you by the chain which I wear; by the sufferings which I offer to God for you. Live so that we may be united in heaven for all eternity. I give you *rendez-vous* there. Adieu. I embrace you with my whole heart. Tell our good Curé and M. Nouard, my friend and benefactor, how constantly I pray for them. Do not forget this.

'Your devoted son and brother,
'BERNEUX.'

He adds a little 'cantique,' of which the refrain is: '*Vive la joie quand même.*'

MM. Berneux and Galy were arrested, as we have seen, on Easter-day, the 11th of April 1841, and conducted to Hué, the chief town of Cochin-China, on the 28th of May following. They were found guilty of having preached the Christian faith, and condemned on this account to be beheaded: the signature of the king to the death-warrant was alone wanting for the execution of the sentence. The young king, Thieu Tri, was not more favourable to the Christians than his father; but he had not as yet received solemn investiture from the Emperor of China; in addition to which he feared to compromise himself with France by putting European missionaries to death. Our generous confessors lived, therefore, between hope and fear. The martyr's glorious recompense appeared ever to fly before them, at the very moment they thought to have attained it. In a letter addressed to Mgr.

Bouvier the 27th Oct. 1842, after seventeen months' imprisonment at Hué, M. Berneux writes:

'A few weeks ago I had the strongest reason to hope that I should be executed at the end of this month or the beginning of next. The edict is not yet published, and it appears that the king intends to wait until next year. May the holy will of God be done! Would that I might profit by this time of preparation!'

In the Divine decrees a martyr's crown was indeed reserved to this generous athlete; but it was not to be won until after long years of suffering and of apostolic labours.

CHAPTER IX.

Arrest of MM. Charrier, Miche, and Duclos. Miseries of the captivity. Christian sympathy. Confessors of Quang-tri. Visit of Philip Phê. Sentence of death; joy of the missionaries. Death-warrant signed, and missionaries removed to the great prison. Execution indefinitely postponed. Description of the prison. Horrors of this captivity.

THE captivity of our missionaries was indefinitely prolonged; and before long, others, who had fallen into the hands of their persecutors, were sent to the capital to become their companions in chains. M. Charrier, who had laboured in Tonquin for eight years, was arrested in October 1841, and condemned to death; but an order coming from the king for his removal to Hué, just as the sentence was about to be put into execution, he joined his brethren on the 26th of the following November. At the commencement of the next year their number was increased by the addition of MM. Miche and Duclos, who had been arrested as they were on the point of leaving Cochin-China for the kingdom of Laos. The accounts which their letters give of this weary period of captivity remind us of those of the early martyrs, and of the devotion of the first Christians; for, indeed, the holy Catholic Church is ever the same in all ages; her children, fortified by supernatural grace, have ever shown a heroism of which our cowardly nature of itself is incapable; and it is this special proof of her divine origin which always produces the greatest effect upon the mind of the heathen.

The prisons which witnessed the sufferings of our missionaries were reserved for the most vicious and degraded of criminals; and those in charge were little removed in character from the prisoners themselves. Their surroundings were consequently of the most painful kind, and doubly bitter to the sight and ears of these pure servants of God, who were compelled to live in such a sink of iniquity. Nevertheless, even these wretched criminals considered themselves at liberty to add what lay in their power to their sufferings. M. Berneux was fortunately located near two mandarin prisoners, and was therefore a little protected from the ill usage of the jailers; but M. Galy was exposed to every brutality. The prisoners, by signs, took delight in expressing the cruel nature of the torments which awaited him. He was exposed, like a wild beast, to the insults of spectators and visitors; but worse than all was the companionship of human creatures who were strangers alike to all sentiments of humanity and decency, and abandoned to every kind of vice.

However, they had moments of consolation from the occasional visits of the Christians, who would risk everything to show them some mark of affection and respect. 'One day two venerable old men made their appearance, who brought us every kind of affectionate message from the Christians, and said that their only regret was not to be allowed to share our captivity. One of them said: "All the churches in Europe have had martyrs for the faith of Christ; we alone have hitherto been deprived of them. Now we hear that you are about to be put to death, and we implore you not to forget us, O fathers, in that heavenly kingdom which you will so soon reach, but to obtain for us by your prayers tranquillity to the Church, and a fresh supply of labourers from the West for our desolate land."' One good creature more especially would come regularly every Sunday under pretext of seeing a relation. Though seated close to M. Berneux, she was unable to exchange a word with him; but through her pretended relation, he learned that she had come from a great distance in order to see the fathers. Through him she contrived to convey to them sometimes a little fruit, sometimes a little money. As she treated the other prisoners and the soldiers with the like generosity, her visits were welcomed by all. Yet whilst she watched them eating, her tears would flow, and the long sighs which escaped her made the missionaries constantly fear that she would be discovered.

But greater consolations than these were in store for them. M. Galy writes thus of one of these most interesting interviews:

'We had witnessed,' says he, 'the triumphs of the three confessors of Quang-tri at their last and probably twentieth examination. We had been unable to make more than a momentary sign of recognition, as we passed out of court to return to our respective prisons, much as we longed to speak to them, and to kiss the chains which they had worn with so much glory and for such a length of time.

'One day our *Cai* made known by signs that a Christian desired to speak with us in a retired part of the prison. We hurried there, and to our joy found Philip Phê, the youngest of the three confessors of Quang-tri. The sight of this young man, whose masculine countenance contrasted agreeably with the gentleness and piety of his words, had the effect upon us of an angelic apparition. He had left his prison under pretext of buying some remedies, accompanied by a Christian soldier. To describe the happiness of this interview would be utterly impossible; it was a foretaste of heaven. The calmness of the youthful confessor was a little troubled at the recital of our sufferings. He related also with deep emotion those of M. Delamotte; but joy lighted up his face again as he spoke rapidly of his own. Then he added, "Heaven is well worth the little tribulations which we suffer in following Jesus Christ, our good Master!" Indeed, the sweet serenity of his face as he spoke excited *us* far more than any words of ours could affect *him*.

'We recommended ourselves to his prayers and to those of his companions, and we separated after having asked of God the favour of being permitted to die the same day. Since then he has frequently come to see us, accompanied by Lorenzo, the good Christian soldier. It was he who brought us the official report of our condemnation to death, which he believed would be executed without delay. Never did words fall more sweetly on our ears than these, " You are to die within three days." In making this announcement he shared our enthusiasm; Lorenzo, the soldier who accompanied him, wept.... Those who might have seen us, without knowing what was passing, would not certainly have taken us for three condemned criminals. When the moment came for separation, Philip's eyes were filled with tears, and his voice failed him. We spoke of our next meeting in heaven; when we promised, if possible, by our prayers to hasten his entrance and that of his glorious companion. Why should we meet again on earth ?'

It was a great trial to our missionaries to have the execution of the sentence indefinitely postponed. One criminal had already been removed for execution, and every moment they thought their turn was come. They had cut their hair close behind, and prepared their best clothes. But these melancholy delays do not appear to have disturbed the serenity of their minds, as they lived in the contemplation of the glorious examples of the patience of the saints, often condemned to a long life of waiting before being put in possession of the object of their desires.

It was at this time that M. Charrier underwent the most cruel tortures, with a courage which even called forth the admiration of his judges. When it was proposed to inflict upon him again the terrible ' rotin,' one of the mandarins exclaimed, ' Of what good would that be? Nothing will conquer those men. Yesterday I gave him eleven strokes, and he seemed only to be asleep.'

As the time of their captivity was prolonged, the patience and courage which they showed under all their varied sufferings appear to have at last touched the hearts of their jailers, who were able to procure for them various indulgences, and likewise to extend their liberty in many ways. At the same time M. Berneux reports that in consequence of the young king not having published any fresh edict against the Christians, a great number of the heathen were brought to confess the faith. But this truce was of short duration. On the 3d of December 1842, king Thieu-Tri signed the death-warrant, with orders, nevertheless, to suspend the execution of the sentence until his pleasure should be farther known. At the commencement of October, MM. Berneux, Galy, and Charrier had been transferred to the prison of condemned criminals; when, on the 7th of December, they were once more joined by their companions MM. Miche and Duclos.

It would be difficult to give an adequate description of the miseries of this prison. The following is taken from the account of M. Miche:

'At the western extremity of the town of Hué, in the midst of uninhabited marshes, rises a vast enclosure about twelve feet high, forming a square of about three hundred feet. These walls are surrounded by ditches filled with water, and surmounted by a palisade of thorny bamboos. Within this enclosure is situated the prison known by the name of Rhâm-Dâng, a true receptacle of vice and crime of every description. Here day by day arrive from every part of the country criminals of every class, many of them real objects of pity. A little bridge of bamboos thrown across the ditches leads to the door, the threshold of which is rarely crossed except in a coffin, or in order to go to execution.

'The half of this enclosure is covered by rice-fields; the remainder is occupied by four great buildings, one of which belongs to our keepers, and the others are the prisons. The first of these is reserved for the great mandarins; the second, in which we reside, contains dignitaries of the second order; as for the third, it receives the lowest of the people.

'These buildings, without walls, without enclosure, are nothing more than vast sheds formed by a multitude of columns supporting a roof covered with tiles. Each of these dwellings is divided into two compartments, one of which is raised four feet above the other. This is a great dark room, or rather an enormous chest, lined with rough planks, into which the light never penetrates; the only opening into it being the door, which is always closed when prisoners are there. During the day all the inmates live on the ground-floor, which is the bare earth; some tattered mats being the only protection against the wind, and which each person must procure for himself. Every prisoner has his own little hovel; and when night comes, at a signal given the company is obliged to mount into the upper story. By a particular favour from the captain, the prisoners of the first and second class are not obliged to change their room; and although we are unable to stand upright in our *hen-roosts*, we are incomparably better off than in the furnace overhead. I believe no

European could live here eighteen months short of a miracle: we are surrounded by marshes; the ground we stand upon is like a sponge. During the rainy season the water reaches our cabins as high as our beds; added to which, heaped as we are the one upon the other, surrounded by more than fifty fires, and always in the midst of smoke, we feel during the hot season as though we were dwelling in a live furnace. The mosquitoes, bugs, and other vermin add greatly to our annoyances. Three times a day we are passed under review. The soldiers arrange us in lines of five, and count us most carefully for fear of an evasion; for in the case of an escaped prisoner, the captain and the sentinels are liable to the same punishment as the fugitive.

'It was, I assure you, no small humiliation when for the first time we found ourselves squatting on the ground amongst thieves and murderers, and elbowed by lepers; but the disciples are not above their Master. Was not Jesus Christ confounded with thieves? was not an assassin preferred before him?'

The Annamite government, M. Miche goes on to relate, certainly provides food for its prisoners, but in an insufficient manner, and the rice is damaged. 'I cannot,' says he, 'describe the terrible spectacle which the third prison presents, and which is only separated from ours by a passage ten feet wide. The first time I ventured in, I saw a whole troop of criminals, loaded with heavy chains, stretched naked upon the wet ground, and abandoned like animals about to yield up their last breath. The stronger ones stood up with difficulty, crying, "Doi! Doi!"

(I am hungry! I am hungry!) Others were too weak to express their misery; but fixing on me an expiring gaze, they revealed more by their silence than if they had been able to express their fearful anguish. During the last month about forty prisoners in this entrenchment died, and the mortality continues. . . .

'After showing you the black side of the picture, it is but just that I should let you see the bright one. We have the joy of being reunited to those confessors of the faith who have preceded us, and to those who followed us here. There are Christians, too, who come from a distance to see us, if not without danger, at least without fear. More than this, we have been honoured by the visit of One infinitely more precious: Jesus Christ Himself has not disdained to visit us in our prison, in order to nourish those who have fought in His cause. The evening before this happy day we heard each other's confession; and the following morning at daybreak a native priest, to whom we had made known our wishes, came, under cover of seeing some acquaintance, to crown our desires. To receive the Body and Blood of Jesus Christ is at all times a happiness to the faithful soul; but to communicate after being ten months deprived of the Holy Sacrifice; to communicate with an iron collar, and a chain borne for the love of Christ Himself; to communicate in a prison, under sentence of death, under the very eyes of our persecutors,—this is a joy which it is impossible for me to express.'

The captive missionaries received, in spite of

all prohibitions, external help, which enabled them to provide for their own wants and those of the Christians who shared their captivity; besides assisting materially those wretched prisoners who, as we have seen, were reduced to the last extremity of misery. The Christians of Cochin-China, though poor and ruined by the persecutions, did what they could; but the Association for the Propagation of the Faith, by their alms, conveyed through the hands of the Vicars-apostolic, provided for the needs of the Christian prisoners; and thus M. Miche adds: 'If we do not also experience the horrors of famine, if we do not sink under our misery like the poor wretches who fall at our side, it is to the liberality of this admirable society that we owe our preservation.'

CHAPTER X.

Their delivery by the prompt and bold measures taken by M. Lévêque, commander of the Héroïne. They are taken on board the Héroïne, and set sail for France. MM. Miche and Duclos are left at Singapore.

For two months M. Berneux and his companions lingered in this frightful captivity, expecting and hoping from day to day that the crown of martyrdom would at length be the reward of their sufferings. At the end of this time, however, they were surprised by a message from the king, begging for an explanation of two thermometers which he had had sent him from Singapore, and desiring to know if they would be willing to undertake the instruction of some native interpreters, of whom he was in great need, on account of his relations with Europeans.

This proposition caused them both surprise and embarrassment; but considering that this new position might afford them opportunities of advancing the cause of Christianity, they agreed to the proposal, under the condition that they were to be removed to a healthy dwelling, that their chains should be taken off, and that they should be left entirely free. If these conditions could not be complied with, they begged to be allowed to remain in peace where they were.

In consequence of this they were at once conveyed to a house spacious and commodious enough for the country; but their chains were not removed, and a guard of six soldiers proved that they were no more at liberty than before. They therefore refused to begin teaching, and even declined the money sent them by the king, notwithstanding the entreaties of the mandarin that they would not delay, and his promises that their desires should soon be complied with. They knew that the removal of their chains was indispensable for the encouragement of the unhappy Christians; and they continued firm in their refusal. Thus they remained for three months, when a French man-of-war unexpectedly arrived, and succeeded in delivering them from their captivity.

M. Lévêque, commander of the corvette Héroïne, soon after his arrival in the bay, became acquainted in a strange manner with all the particulars relating to the captivity of the missionaries. The officers went daily on shore to a little island to amuse themselves by hunting monkeys, when their attention was drawn to an Annamite, who, concealed amongst the bushes, endeavoured, by making the sign of the Cross, to discover himself to them without being seen by his countrymen. They found indeed that he was a Christian, bearing a letter to the commander of the Héroïne, and giving an account of the long sufferings of the Christian missionary priests, whose very existence in the country had been positively denied. The assertions of the mandarins to the contrary had therefore no effect upon the captain. Refusing all their friendly offers, he demanded at their hands the five captive missionaries, and threatened to remain there six months in case of a refusal.

It was with great difficulty that the mandarin was persuaded to forward the letter containing this demand to the king; but when it was received, it had the desired effect. The king, Thieu-Tri, was not as yet firmly established on his throne, and he feared above everything a war with France. The bold and energetic demeanour of the commander of the Héroïne decided him to release our generous confessors of the faith; and 'on the 12th of March,' writes M. Charrier, 'our deliverance was accomplished. On the same day the king published a manifesto, in which he announced that the king of our country, informed of the charges laid against us, had sent a *savage mandarin* humbly to intreat the pardon of the king of Cochin-China!

'A numerous escort accompanied us from the capital as far as the port. Having arrived at Touranne, we halted at the house of the mandarin, in order to hear the royal manifesto, which directed us to be given up to the commander of the Héroïne. Here M. Lévêque received us, at the head of his officers, in great pomp. As we approached the coast between a double file of soldiers, an immense crowd of pagans and neophytes looked on in silent astonishment at our deliverance. At three o'clock on the afternoon of the 17th we were on board the Héroïne, and the following morning at eight o'clock we set sail.

'During the night an Annamite bark crept furtively alongside, through the midst of the junks which covered the bay. It was manned by neophytes, who, at the peril of their lives, came to reclaim their missionaries, and to place in the hands of the commander a letter from Mgr. Cuenot, begging him to land us on the south coast, where a ship would be in readiness to take us back to our several missions. But in vain. We were obliged to bid farewell, with a fervent blessing, to our adopted country, leaving behind us our proscribed brethren, our persecuted children, and the chains which we had hoped never to put off except at the gate of heaven.

'At Singapore we again implored M. Lévêque to let us go back to our missions, and were supported in our request by our brethren in that town. But M. Lévêque signified to us, that having reclaimed us from the king of Cochin-China in the name of his government, he could not listen to such a proposal. Nevertheless our entreaties so far prevailed, as to induce him to consent to leave MM. Miche and Duclos at Singapore; the former being appointed to direct the Chinese college of Pulopenang, the latter being too weak to bear a longer sea-voyage.'

The other missionaries were, in spite of their long sufferings, in tolerable health; and the care bestowed upon them by the commander and officers of the Héroïne is mentioned by them in their correspondence in terms of the deepest gratitude.

CHAPTER XI.

Voyage to Bourbon. M. Berneux obtains permission from the governor to return to Macao. He is appointed to Mandchouria. Journey and arrival.

It was with great sorrow that M. Berneux now found himself about to return home without having done anything for his mission. But M. Lévêque was consistent in his refusal, as he had received the missionaries from the king of Cochin-China on condition that they should not set foot again either in Cochin-China or Tonquin. The voyage continued, therefore, and after three months they arrived at the island of Bourbon.

Here, however, M. Berneux met with more success; for, on renewing his petition to the governor, he informed Mgr. Bouvier that the governor of the isle of Bourbon had allowed him to return to Macao, but only after a promise that he should not enter the territory of the king of Cochin-China. 'It was,' he adds, 'a condition very hard to accept;' but, considering that he would probably meet with as little success should he appeal to the government at home, and considering also the expense, loss of time, and uncertainty which would be the result of a return to France, he accepted the governor's proposal, and gave up for ever the cherished mission of Tonquin.

The sight of this missionary, hardly escaped from

the frightful prisons of Cochin-China, and bearing still on his body the glorious scars of the battles fought for the honour of Jesus Christ, yet imploring, as the most precious boon, the permission to devote himself again to his apostolic labours, produced a profound impression upon every one on board. Many years afterwards, one who accompanied him on his voyage back wrote, upon hearing of his martyrdom: 'Never have I known a man with a nobler soul, with a more generous heart, or one more passionately devoted to the glory of God and the salvation of his fellow-creatures.'

From Singapore to Macao M. Berneux, with three other missionaries, made the voyage in the Alcmène, and during the transit, which was performed in fifteen days, they had the opportunity of making a little mission which was full of interest to them. Hardly had they got on board, when some of the sailors begged to be prepared for their first communion. The time being short, not an instant was lost. The whole day they were occupied in teaching the catechism and the long-forgotten prayers. Of these brave fellows, those who could read assisted those who could not; and the result was so satisfactory, that in ten or twelve days they were sufficiently instructed to receive their first communion.

'On the 17th of August the commander Desplantes,' says M. Berneux, 'himself prepared us an altar in his own room. I celebrated holy Mass, at which about twenty sailors communicated. The commandant and his staff assisted. It was indeed a feast-day for the whole crew. After the service, many sailors who had hesitated at first came to be instructed, but it was too late: we were on the point of arriving at Macao.'

After waiting for two months at Macao, M. Berneux was appointed to the new mission of Mandchouria, which had been just given to the charge of Mgr. Verolles, and where European missionaries were entirely unknown.

The passage from Hong-kong to the isle of Chusan was a painful and a perilous one for M. Berneux. The English ship in which he sailed was out of repair, and for three weeks he was unable from sickness to leave his berth, although the sea came in and flooded his cabin. At a league from Chusan the ship was thrown by the violence of the storm between two rocks, and was only saved from her frightful position by an officer and fourteen sailors belonging to a man-of-war stationed at Chusan. Another accident followed soon after, and M. Berneux took refuge in a Chinese boat, which landed him safely on shore. Being desirous of leaving Chusan at once, he made many ineffectual efforts to be taken on board one of the English ships trading from Chusan to Shanghai; but at last despairing of getting a passage in a European vessel, he resolved to embark in a little Chinese junk, and thus to abandon himself entirely to the care of Divine Providence. He was on the point of embarking, when he heard that an English ship just setting sail would receive him willingly, and he arrived without accident at Shanghai.

The most interesting portion of his voyage, however, was that between Nankin and Leao-tong, which was made in a Chinese ship almost entirely manned by Christians. 'This passage of a month,' he writes, 'has amply repaid me for all my previous fatigues. . . . Every day I was able to celebrate holy Mass; evening and morning we had prayers and rosary— it was almost like the life of the seminary. Their profession was no excuse with these Christians for dispensing with fasts and abstinences; and three times a week, when the navigation permitted, we made the Stations of the Cross.

'A few days after our departure, the wind being contrary, we cast anchor near an island where 18 Christian barks awaited a favourable wind. Hearing that we were on board, these Christians came in great numbers every morning in order to be present at holy Mass. On Ash Wednesday more than one hundred and twenty Christians received the ashes upon the deck of the junk, upon which the altar was dressed.

'At length, on the 15th March, we landed at Leao-tong, the new mission, to which the will of God has called me to work for the salvation of souls. I had yet sixty leagues of land-journey to reach the residence of the Vicar-apostolic, Mgr. Verolles. I therefore hired a wagon and five horses to convey myself and my two couriers over the mountains which we had to cross. This journey, which occupied six days, through an entirely pagan country, was not accomplished without difficulty. Two things betrayed my European extraction—my ignorance of the language and my red moustache.

'Our couriers obviated the first of these difficulties by passing me off as a merchant from Kiang-Nan, where a language is spoken which is unknown in the other provinces. The other was remedied by a daily application of ink; and in this manner I arrived peacefully at my destination, blessing God, who had thus protected me during my long and perilous journey.'

The health of M. Berneux began to suffer from the effects of so many journeys and fatigues, following so closely upon the sufferings of a long captivity. The necessity of mastering the Mandchou language before beginning his missionary labours, now afforded him the rest he so much needed, and allowed him to regain his strength a little.

In a letter dated the 27th March 1844, some days after his arrival in Mandchouria, M. Berneux expresses his regret at having been obliged to spend so much time in travelling, and at the years which he had been deprived of the happiness of preaching the gospel to the heathen. 'It will be truly said of me,' he writes, 'that I have come on the mission only to travel from one country to another, and to make a course of practical geography, rather than to work for the glory of God and the salvation of souls.' Although destined by God to bear the gospel to other countries than this, it yet pleased Him to allow him to remain eleven years in Mandchouria, being one half of his apostolic career.

CHAPTER XII.

Mandchouria. Divisions: 1. Ghirin-Oula. 2. Sakhalien. 3. Leao-Tong. Climate. Poverty. Chinese element. Religions. Superstitions.

WE will now give some account of the country which was to be the scene of M. Berneux's fresh labours. Mandchouria is bounded on the north by Siberia; on the west by Mongolia; on the south-west by China; on the south by the Corea; and on the east by the sea of Japan. It is divided into three provinces—1. Ghirin-Oula; 2. Sakhalien-Oula; 3. Leao-Tong.

1. The province of Ghirin-Oula is, generally speaking, flat and woody, and very cold. It is the place to which Chinese criminals are transported, and contains but four badly-built towns surrounded by mud walls. The chief town is Ghirin-Oula, upon the left bank of the Soungari. The exiles, who are the principal inhabitants of this place, are generally engaged in the search for 'gen-seng,' which is much thought of by the Chinese, and which grows here in abundance. The moral degradation of these unfortunate creatures is much on a par with their physical miseries. The details given by missionaries of the melancholy and hopeless lives of these people,

and the hardships of their mode of existence, almost surpass belief. Wild untrodden forests—beasts of prey—gigantic trees—frightful winters—all would seem to preclude hope to the wretched outcasts who are condemned to roam there, or who have fled thither to be out of the reach of justice.

2. The province of Sakhalien is the most extensive of the three. Although the climate is extremely cold, and the winters are long and rigorous, nevertheless the soil is not particularly barren. The Emperor of China keeps up a few weak garrisons on the frontier, and a kind of trade is carried on with the savages, who bring skins in exchange for tea and the manufactured productions of the Chinese empire. Almost all these native tribes prefer a wandering to a settled life. In speaking of this territory, M. Berneux sums it up as 'a vast desert, where neither wood, water, nor wild beasts are wanting; but where it can hardly be said that man exists.' It appears that the Mandchourian simply occupies it in order to prevent other tribes of the north from descending into these vast and all but desert regions. The inhabitants live entirely on hunting and fishing.

3. Leao-Tong is the principal seat of the Catholic missions, and certainly the most important province of Mandchouria, both on account of its population and its vicinity to Pekin. The capital is Moukden, and contains within itself two towns; the inner one being occupied by the imperial palace and all the dwellings of the government officials, whilst the exterior is inhabited by merchants and all who have no employment under government.

The population is estimated at not less than 200,000 souls.

Every emperor is under the necessity of visiting Moukden once in the course of his reign, for the purpose of venerating the remains of his ancestors. He offers sacrifices and libations with great pomp and ceremony in order to propitiate their souls, who are supposed to have become infernal spirits. Every ten years the portrait of the emperor is sent to *visit* these his distant possessions: it happened that the year of M. Berneux's arrival this famous portrait was expected. One of the first princes of the blood carried it upon a magnificently ornamented car. It is adored—sacrifices are offered to it; and what surpasses all our European ideas upon such a subject, a road is built expressly for it from fifteen to eighteen feet wide, and raised in the middle of the high road, all the way from Pekin to Moukden.

The conquest of China has occasioned the emigration of the noblest of the Mandchou families, who have followed their princes. On the other hand, the Chinese have, as it were, made a pacific conquest of the people. In Mandchouria, and above all in Leao-Tong, the language, customs, and even the religion are Chinese, although the two races are not, as yet, amalgamated; and the very first question asked of a stranger is, whether he be Chinese or Mandchou?

As for the climate, although in the same latitude as Naples and the south of Italy, Mandchouria is far from enjoying the same mild temperature. For nine months the cold is extreme, and the heat for the other three proportionately great. The deepest rivers in winter are frozen, and the ice is eight or ten feet thick; it is the same with the gulf of Leao-Tong. 'I have myself,' says Mgr. Verolles, 'wandered over these icy solitudes. There are enormous icebergs heaped together like so many rocks, and offering at a distance the view of an immense plain covered with ruins; and this sea nevertheless is in the same latitude as the bay of Naples.'

On the 28th of October 1844 M. Berneux writes to Mgr. Bouvier:

'Your lordship knows something of the cold of these countries. Usually it is 25° to 30° Reaumer, and even 40° in the northern part of the mission... The houses have no fireplaces, but a kind of oven, upon which one sleeps, eats, and works. In travelling, it is necessary to be clothed in furs from head to foot. My winter costume consists of a woollen hat, a tunic lined with fox-skin, trousers and boots of the same, a fur cravat, and a fur bag for my nose and ears, regardless of the grotesque appearance of such a decoration... Notwithstanding,' he adds in a letter to his sister, 'that I suffer very much from the cold, God's grace enables the missionary to adapt himself to all, and to be happy everywhere.'

In addition to this rigorous climate, the inhabitants, and especially the Christians, suffer severely from poverty and insufficient nourishment.

'In the Christian village,' says he, 'where I have been studying the language this summer, all the nourishment these poor people are able to procure consists of a few roots. The missionary helps them a little; but his own resources are scanty enough. One of the delicacies of the country are the silkworms, which are cooked whole in their cocoons, and come out, of course, like great black worms; which,' M. Berneux owns, 'are more likely to take away one's appetite than to excite it.'

The principal food of the missionaries seems to have been millet, rice, radishes, and a kind of cabbage; meat is rare, although every kind is eaten. Dogs and cats are reserved for great feasts.

But the rarest and most valuable product in Mandchouria is the *gen-seng*, which is a wonderful tonic, and very superior to quinine. It grows wild, and only the root is used; but it is very dear. A piece of this root is soaked for about a month in some white wine, and then taken in small quantities. Its effects are marvellous; and people in the last stage of weakness have been perfectly cured by it.

The superstitions of the country vary in the different provinces. In the north they consist of the grossest idolatry and the worship of evil spirits. In Leao-Tong the Chinese have imported their own religions: 1. The philosophical pantheism of Confucius. 2. A kind of polytheism, in which worship is offered to the skies, to the genii of the earth and of the stars, to the souls of deceased relations, over all of which a supreme being is recognised, whom they call the Emperor of Heaven. The 3d religion is a modification of Buddhism, imported from India. The priests of this religion, having neglected the study of their own peculiar philosophy, teach a kind of idolatry, which is externally represented by a great number of religious ceremonies in their temples, and by monstrous allegorical figures. This religion has its hermits and its anchorites, living in the caves of the mountains.

'That the devil plays a very active part in pagan countries, and over the actions of the heathen,' says Mgr. Verolles, 'thousands of facts are constantly proving. Amongst them there is one which is as common in China as it is in Mandchouria, and which is attested by innumerable witnesses. Should a woman, in consequence of bitter words with her husband, or blows, or any other cause, desire to put an end to her life (and the case is frequent enough in this empire), there is no occasion to hang herself. The unfortunate creature places herself in her chair, passes the fatal rope round her neck, and he who was a homicide from the beginning undertakes the rest—he draws the knot.'

The following is the description of Mgr. Verolles of one of the superstitions among these people. The Chinese, inflated as they are with their own supposed wisdom, are ready at the same time to believe the greatest absurdities; and in this all idolaters, of whatever sort, are consistent.

'Towards the latter end of the year all the gods, of whatever kind, are supposed to quit the earth, in order to pass a short vacation in heaven. As a preparation for their departure, every one places on his domestic altar a little hay and some millet, as a provision for the horse which is about to bear the immortal deity through the upward road leading to the skies. As for himself, in order that he should not be able to answer too many questions of his celestial brethren concerning the household he has left behind, and which generally does not bear close inspection, his mouth is carefully glued up with gum and sugar, and he is wished a good journey; after which his image is burnt, and he is so dismissed to the other world.'

Another missionary describes the return of these deities:

'The moment being arrived (which is midnight), men, women, children, old and young, every one, in fact, turns out into the middle of the court-yard, each dressed in his best. The father of the family, who alone has the privilege of seeing these invisible gods, moves his eyes from point to point of the heavens, until they appear to him; then indicating the spot, he exclaims, "They are coming—on your knees!" All the assembly, including the horses and carriages, are turned towards them. They prostrate themselves towards the point indicated, and thus receive their divinities; after which they return to their houses, and give themselves up to every kind of feasting in their honour.'

We smile at these absurd superstitions; but when we reflect that even in our own land the invocation of spirits, and what is called 'spiritualism,' is so widely practised and believed, can we wonder at the errors of those poor people, or cease to thank God, who has preserved us, by the teaching of His Church, from such marvellous follies?

CHAPTER XIII.

Commencement of missionary labours in Mandchouria. Account of M. Berneux's manner of teaching.

TOWARDS the latter end of the sixteenth century, P. Ricci, S.J., succeeded in introducing the Christian faith into China, in the very midst of the imperial made the conquest of China, received the Fathers court. The Mandchou emperor, who had lately very favourably, admiring as much the wisdom as the virtue of the holy missioners. The relations between the court of Pekin and that of Mandchouria were too intimate for the faith not to find its way into these remote countries, which for a long period acknowledged the jurisdiction of the Vicar-apostolic of Pekin. It was in 1838 that the Holy See separated Mandchouria from the diocese of Pekin, and placed Mgr. Verolles at the head of the new see, where he arrived in the spring of 1841, accompanied by one priest, M. Ferreol, who was only waiting for an opportunity of introducing himself into the Corea. He found everything had to be begun again, owing to the revolutions which the country had undergone, and which had almost obliterated every trace of the missionary labours which had preceded him. Towards the close of the year 1846 he was joined by several other priests, and amongst them was M. Berneux.

He thus gives an account of the commencement of his work: 'In the month of December last I set out on my first trial of arms. I could only stammer a little of the terrible jargon of the celestial empire; but the need was so urgent, that I was obliged to make up my mind to serve some of the stations. The following is our mode of proceeding. After the harvest has been gathered in, and when a degree of cold of about twenty degrees has frozen the most rapid of the rivers, the missionary starts for his campaign. The Christians being previously advertised, are all ready to receive him; and the richest, or rather the least poor, inhabitant of the village prepares a room for the reception of the Father. This room becomes the church, for here the missionary says Mass, preaches, &c.

'The day after his arrival he begins, by celebrating Mass before daybreak. As they have no clocks, and there is no means of calling them together, they arrive often in the middle of the night, for fear of losing Mass, and assemble with much noise, so that sleep is impossible. . . . Poor people! this is generally the only time in the year when they can hear Mass, and they appreciate the grace in proportion to its rarity. After Mass and a short instruction, the priest enters the confessional, where he remains until two or three o'clock in the afternoon. The remainder of the day is occupied in conversing with catechists and others, . . . and thus passes each day. When all the confessions have been heard, he passes on to another station, where everything is conducted in the same manner. Every station is supplied with catechists, who superintend the prayers, which are said in common on Sundays and feast-days. The men have their own chapel, the women theirs. During the four months of my visitation this year I have heard about nine hundred confessions, and baptised about one hundred and fifty adult pagans. This is in addition to a great number of pagan children, in danger of death, who have been baptised by the catechists. We have men whom we employ to go from village to village as doctors. They have medicines, which they give away gratis, and when they find a child very sick they baptise it.'

He writes to his mother on the 17th June 1849: 'You did not know your son was a great horseman, did you? But I assure you, I am become quite a proficient in that line. I rode the other day one hundred and fifty leagues to give the last sacraments to a sick man, and was not at all exhausted, though the heat was excessive. But the work here is incessant, from the great distances the missionary has to traverse; my whole life is spent in hearing confessions and teaching the Catechism. I have not a moment to read the books I brought from Europe. My Bible and my *Imitation* are my only companions. Would to God that I practised the lessons those two books contain! I should soon become a saint, and my work for the sanctification of souls would then really prosper. I hope you pray a great deal for me, and ask of God to change my corrupt nature, that I may become *really* what now I only *seem* to be.'

In 1847, M. Berneux gives some farther details of missionary life in Mandchouria. 'I have now been six months absent from home—that spot, I should say, where I can take a little rest. Of this, however, I have had none for two years. The administration of the Sacraments and teaching occupies every instant of every day. I hear confessions during the day; I pray during the night; I take my recreation on horseback, journeying from station to station. ... God proportions my strength to my need, and I am in better health than I used to be in France. ... During the past six months I have heard nearly two thousand confessions, and travelled across rivers, and over mountains and glaciers, about five hundred and fifty leagues. I have yet nearly one thousand confessions to hear. I work a great deal, but the main point is to work well. I entreat you to ask it very frequently of our Lord for me.'

During the ten years of his residence in Mandchouria he speaks of his work being principally amongst the Christians, and that conversions from paganism were rare. One great means of grace amongst a people with whom infanticide is an ordinary practice was drawn from this very custom. The children exposed by their parents were constantly rescued, or even purchased, by the missionary; and in this manner he says, 'I have founded a little family, whom I hope to bring up in the love of God. ... I have but little money, but I do not fear; it is God's work, and He will take care of it.' These children were a great solace to him, and repaid his care by their docility and devotion. In 1849, twelve hundred of these little innocents were thus saved, and two thousand the following year. In another letter Mgr. Berneux speaks with delight of a little child he had just bought: 'In three months he has learnt all his prayers, and can say the Catechism perfectly; yet he is only six years old! His greatest pleasure is in prayer. Not for all the world would he eat without saying his "Benedicite." The other day he was sent to an orphanage a few miles off. He was to breakfast at an inn on the way; and there, to the great astonishment of everybody, when breakfast was announced, this little fellow knelt down and said his little prayers out loud, making at the same time a great sign of the Cross. You can't think the joy this child gives me. To-morrow I am going to baptise him.'

Travelling was at all times dangerous in these parts, owing to the hordes of banditti who infested the roads. On one occasion M. Berneux fell into the hands of one of these hordes. He was travelling in a wagon in the depth of winter, when nine men, mounted on horseback, took possession of him, and took from him his fox's skin. Being perplexed at the sight of his ornaments and Breviary, they questioned him, and finding him to be a missionary, and that he taught the religion of the King of Heaven, they restored his mantle, saying, 'Why did you not tell us sooner that you were the *Llama* (priest)? for we would not have stopped the wagon!' The chief, who was a Jew, then called the rest of his band, and ordered them not to touch anything that belonged to him; and in a few minutes the party had dispersed, not, however, without so far disobeying their chief's orders as to take his pipe and tobacco, and the six hundred francs which were his provision for a year! A little farther on, they pillaged eight other wagons.'

CHAPTER XIV.

Threatening persecution. Prompt measures taken by the Bishop and M. Berneux. Peace is restored. He is raised to the Episcopate, and appointed Vicar-Apostolic of the Corea.

FROM the first the mission in Mandchouria had been allowed to proceed in peace; but in the year 1849 a circumstance occurred which threatened the most serious consequences. The hatred of a pagan for the catechist, in whose house the Bishop and M. Berneux usually resided, induced him to try to injure the catechist by taking possession of his guests, and bringing them before the courts of law. M. Berneux was on a mission at the time, about thirty leagues distant from Mgr. Verolles.

A troop of pagans surrounded his oratory, as the latter was hearing confessions. Seizing his servant (who being Chinese had confronted the assailants), they retired for a time; but on finding they had mistaken their victim, they released the servant, and hastened back to catch Mgr. Verolles. With great difficulty, and by means of a fine Tartar horse, the Bishop contrived to make his escape.

The following morning the mandarin came himself with his satellites, and arrested all the Christians they could find. Six neophytes and a catechumen were loaded with irons, and put to the question. The catechumen apostatised, and an aged man followed his example; the rest confessed their faith boldly in spite of the torture.

The Mandchou Christians, naturally very timid, were thrown into the utmost consternation by these proceedings; the women alone remained in the villages, the men fled in every direction. It was of the utmost importance to reassure them; and M. Berneux was, as Vicar-general, charged with the management of this unfortunate affair. As soon therefore as he heard the account of what had taken place, he started for Moukden. There, without touching on the subject of religion, he boldly accused their accusers. A mandarin, whose goodwill was dearly bought, promised him a complete triumph. Their position, however, was critical; many writs of arrest were out against their persons, and the stations were filled with alarm, owing to the spies who had been sent in every direction. It was deemed expedient, therefore, to allow the storm to pass for a time; and on the 20th of April they took refuge in a Christian vessel bound for Kiang-Nan. They found a generous supporter in the French consul at Shanghai, M. de Montigny, who wrote to the authorities at Moukden, complaining of the treatment which the Christians had received, and threatening, if justice were not done, to lay an information against them before the French government.

As soon, therefore, as the state of affairs appeared to change for the better, M. Berneux returned to his flock; while Mgr. Verolles took his departure for

Europe. He had earnestly wished M. Berneux to accompany him to recruit his health by a short visit to his native country: but this generous and devoted apostle refused so natural a consolation. He wrote on the subject as follows:

'I should indeed have rejoiced to have come home for a few weeks and to have seen you all again. But this joy would have been too dearly bought. I should have had to abandon for at least a twelvemonth all my dear neophytes, at the very moment when a persecution was likely to break out, which would be doubly trying to their timid nature. To go and to return would have cost ten thousand francs, and I have not eighty at my disposal! No; let us be generous in our sacrifices. The time of recompense will come when we shall be for ever reunited in the bosom of our dear Lord and Master.'

Soon after this, the death of his mother induced his sister to renew her entreaties that he would come home for a time; to which proposal his superiors were even anxious he should consent, feeling how much their fervent missionary was in need of rest. But again he refused, and writes to his sister: 'You would resign yourself more easily to our separation if you could only realise how useful a priest is in these regions, and how many souls are lost for want of one. I am only now beginning to see the fruit of my labours for the salvation of these people, who have learned to confide in and love me, and whose language and customs I have at last mastered. How could I abandon them, and be responsible for all the losses of grace which my absence might entail?'

Little is known for some years after this of the labours of the missionaries in Mandchouria. Some missions were attempted to be formed in the province of Ghirin Oula; but the pagans denounced them, and they were obliged to leave their new stations just as the faith was beginning to take root; and thus the work was arrested for a long period of time in this province. M. Berneux also had two severe illnesses. At one time he was nearly carried off by typhoid fever, and at another by cholera, by which attacks his constitution was thoroughly shaken, although he resumed his work as soon as his strength permitted.

For some time M. Berneux had been the Pro-vicar-Apostolic of Mandchouria, but his humility prevented him from assuming the titles which appertained to him, and which were necessary if he were to be chosen as co-adjutor. Nevertheless the choice of the Holy Father, as well as that of Mgr. Verolles, fell on him, as the one most worthy by his ardent zeal, his remarkable talents, and his confession of the faith, of this honourable distinction. On the 27th of December 1854, accordingly, he received episcopal consecration at the hands of Mgr. Verolles, under the title of Bishop of Tremita. Notwithstanding all the care taken to keep the day of his consecration secret, a great number of neophytes assembled from all parts of the mission to witness this touching ceremony. It was feared that so great a concourse of people would draw upon them some annoyance on the part of the mandarin; but it pleased God that all should go off quietly.

'Poor things,' writes Mgr. Berneux, speaking of this assembly of Christians on the day of his consecration,—'Poor things! they were but too well pleased to see me made a bishop, little doubting that I should ever leave them. Little indeed did I myself imagine it! nevertheless, in the counsels of God my mission to Mandchouria was already finished. Bulls from Rome had already arrived appointing me Bishop of Capse, and Vicar-Apostolic of Corea.'

The self-abnegation of Mgr. Berneux, and his perfect submission to the will of God, are truly sublime. He was about to quit a mission where for eleven years he had worked with such unparalleled success; with whose languages and customs he had become familiar, and amongst a flock who had always shown him the greatest confidence and attachment. And he was about to undertake a totally new mission; in a country of which he knew neither the language nor the customs; to enter on the post of honour of the Catholic apostolate: for suffering of every description and the almost certainty of martyrdom is all that she offers to the missioner in the Corea. 'Corea!' he exclaimed, 'that land of martyrs! Corea, whose name alone causes every fibre of the missionary's heart to vibrate! how could any one refuse to enter it when the doors were open to him!'

God, however, seemed at first to have been satisfied with the goodwill of His servant. A long and dangerous illness, which lasted for eight months, compelled the new bishop to write again to the Holy See, and to implore permission to remain and end his days in Mandchouria, and give up into younger hands the awful and important charge which had been assigned to him.

We do not know whether this letter ever received an answer. All we do know is, that in the month of September 1855, feeling his health partially re-established, he determined no longer to delay his departure for the Corea. 'I know that many difficulties and sufferings await me there,' was his reply to those who urged him to delay till an answer could be received from Rome. 'But these considerations do not move me. I am better, and able to start; so that my simple duty is to go where I have been sent. It is surely the will of God, and to do that will is my sole desire. I only pray for one thing—the grace to fulfil aright the grave obligations which have been laid upon me.'

The Corea is partly bounded by Mandchouria; but such is the vigilance of the frontier guard, that the new prelate found it impossible to enter it by land. He embarked therefore for Shanghai, in the month of September 1855, in spite of his horror of the sea, which he confesses with the greatest simplicity; and on the 17th January following, he quitted Shanghai, on board a Chinese bark, and directed his course towards his new and cherished mission of Corea. It will be as well, however, before entering upon the details of this perilous voyage, to give our readers a brief outline of the history of the Catholic Church in the Corea, which will indeed be but that of one long and glorious martyrology.

CHAPTER XV.

Corea. Christianity introduced by the Japanese about the end of the sixteenth century. Success. The faith proclaimed publicly even before the arrival of a priest. First persecution. The first missionary, a young Chinese priest, gives himself up in 1801. Mgr. Bruguière offers himself (1833) for the work: his death two years after.

THE Catholic faith appears to have made its way for the first time into the Corea about the end of the sixteenth century, by means of the Japanese, who at that time invaded the country. The commander-in-chief and many of the soldiers being ardent Christians, they carried with them the faith they themselves had received, amongst the people they conquered. About sixty years after, Christianity again re-appeared under very remarkable circumstances. A young Corean of noble birth, named Li, being at Pekin with his father, and desiring to study mathematics, applied to the missionaries for instruction. The consequence of his intercourse with them was his entire conversion; and becoming in his turn an apostle to his own people, he preached with such effect, that not only were his own relations and friends amongst his first disciples, but so great was the success of his preaching, that in less than five years the Christians in the royal city and the adjacent country numbered four thousand.

Religion was publicly proclaimed; but in 1788, a Christian by name Thomas King was arrested, and at once many neophytes presented themselves before the governor, declaring their faith. Astonished at their numbers, the governor sent them back to their homes; whilst Thomas King was condemned to exile, in which he died the same year.

All this time, it is to be remarked that the Corean Christians had no priests, and consequently no sacraments. Many difficulties with regard to faith and observances arose, on which account they resolved to depute Paul Li to wait on the Bishop of Pekin, and ask his advice. He returned with the answers to their questions, and made them farther acquainted with the happiness he had experienced in receiving the sacraments, and assisting in the ceremonies of the Church. The Coreans were in consequence anxious above all to have priests, and again sent a deputation to the Bishop for this purpose. He received their request with joy, and promised to send them a priest, whom they would meet on the frontier in a spot appointed for the purpose.

In the meantime a persecution had arisen, in consequence of the refusal of two Christian families of distinction to join in the pagan ceremonies. When the priest arrived in 1791, no one was there to meet him. At his death in 1794, a young Chinese priest succeeded him; and to the inexpressible joy of the Christians, the sacraments were at last, and for the first time, administered amongst them; so that on Easter-day the number of communicants rejoiced the heart of the missionary.

As soon as the government became acquainted with the introduction of the stranger missionary, an inquisition was set on foot. A holy native Christian woman named Colomba offered him a hiding-place at the peril of her life, where he remained concealed for three years: her charity and zeal were rewarded by the crown of martyrdom. The priest being in safe hiding, three Christians were taken, and being silent before the tribunals, were condemned to be tortured to death. This cruel sentence was executed in all its rigour, and the holy martyrs expired under the hands of their tormenters.

The king did not, however, command a general persecution; but he exiled many Christians, and permitted the governors of the different provinces to annoy them according to their caprice. A few apostatised; but the greater part stood firm, and sacrificed everything for their faith.

At the death of the king in 1800, the number of solid conversions was reckoned at ten thousand. Those mandarins who were opposed to the introduction of the Christian faith took advantage of the weakness of the queen-regent, to raise a general persecution, which soon became very violent. All the Christian mandarins were arrested, and every Christian they could find was imprisoned. So many persons of all ranks and conditions expired under the most frightful tortures, that this persecution is considered by all to have surpassed everything of the kind since the world began.

It was very difficult for the missionary to escape the vigilance of his persecutors. Hunted from place to place, he at length resolved to deliver himself up, which he did in 1801. He was condemned to death; and on the Sunday of the feast of the blessed Trinity (21st May 1801) he was led to execution on a straw barrel in the midst of the troops, all of whom were under arms. The holy confessor preached Jesus Christ to all as he passed. 'I die,' said he, 'for the religion of the God of heaven. Ten years hence a great calamity will befal you, and then you will remember me.' These words, and other phenomena which occurred at the moment of his death, produced a great impression on the heathen, many of whom openly declared his innocence. Then kneeling down and joining his hands, the saint-like missionary received his death-blow with the greatest calmness.

For thirty years again the Corean Church remained without priests. In vain the Christians appealed to the nearest Chinese bishops. The French revolution at the time caused a great dearth of means, and this, added to the difficulty of entering into the Corea, prevented their wishes from being granted. At length in 1832, Mgr. Bruguière, co-adjutor of the Vicar-apostolic of Siam, offered himself for the dangerous and difficult task; and he was appointed Vicar-apostolic of this new church, which was thenceforward confided to the priests of the Missions Etrangères.

Mgr. Bruguière was entirely without resources; he was therefore compelled to borrow the money which was to convey him from Siam to Manilla. At Macao he received a small sum from the Propagation of the Faith, and with these slender means he undertook to cross China, and to enter into the Corea. He went through unheard-of fatigues, and had to surmount obstacles without number; but the physical sufferings he endured were not to be compared to his mental distress caused by the timidity both of his guides and of his hosts. 'I cannot cease to be astonished,' wrote an eye-witness, 'when I think how a European missionary, without any knowledge of the language, and almost without a guide, has travelled through China, sometimes on foot, sometimes mounted on an ass, or in an uncovered cart, and entered into the very midst of the imperial city without being discovered. This is a feat unheard of in the country.' The writer adds, 'he is the first European who has penetrated into Pekin without an imperial diploma. I attribute his special protection to the prayers of the members of the Propagation of the Faith. As long as they plead for us, we are sure of victory.'

Mgr. Bruguière arrived at Cham-Si, on the frontier of Mongol Tartary, in October 1833. But the fatigues of his journey had exhausted the strength of this noble servant of God: two years after he fell ill and died quite suddenly, assisted in his last moments by a Chinese priest who accompanied him. More fortunate than his Vicar-apostolic, F. P. Li, this Chinese priest, who had been educated at Naples, accomplished his entrance into the Corea, and soon after procured the means of admitting MM. Maubant and Chastan. They were the first European missionaries who trod that soil which in a few years they were destined to water with their blood.

CHAPTER XVI.

In 1839 Mgr. Imbert gives himself up with his priests to death. The family Tschoez. Mgr. Ferréol in 1845: Illness and death in 1853. Mgr. Berneux.

MGR. IMBERT had been appointed by the Holy See as coadjutor of Mgr. Bruguière. On his arrival in Mandchouria he learned the death of his Vicar-apostolic; but after many unheard-of dangers he succeeded in passing the Corean frontier, and installed himself in the very capital of the kingdom. This was on the 31st of December 1837. The presence of the prelate and the missionaries could not be long kept secret. A frightful persecution broke out in 1839; and Mgr. Imbert, in order to save his poor Christians, who were most barbarously tortured in order to induce them to disclose his hiding-place, resolved to give himself up, and desired his two companions to do the same. This they did with joy; and the three received together the glorious crown of martyrdom on the 21st of September 1839.

Amongst the most illustrious victims of this persecution were the members of a family called Tschoez. The circumstances of their martyrdom have been related by P. Thomas Tschoez, a Corean priest, and son of Francis, the head of this noble family, who, having left all for the sake of practising their religion in greater security, had taken refuge in forests and mountains, blessing God for the poverty and sufferings which they endured. Although but little instructed, Francis received, through constant meditation and reading of divine things, such an ardent charity, and such wonderful knowledge of the mysteries of the faith, that the Christians would crowd round him to listen to his words, whilst the most obstinate of the pagans were obliged to yield to his arguments. In times of persecution or public calamity Francis was ever ready to comfort and assist his brethren by his words and example, exhorting them at least to patience when he could not relieve their sufferings by his charity. The harvests one year were entirely destroyed by a great inundation; a fearful famine followed, and every one was in despair. Francis alone remained calm and unmoved. 'Why' (he would say to the faithful), 'why do you thus give yourselves up to misery? Are not all human events in the hands of God? If you acknowledge that He is your Father and you His children, why cannot you conform yourselves to His will? After all, how short are all our sufferings here compared to eternity!'

At the same time he multiplied himself to alleviate the misery around him, and by his superhuman charity saved the lives of hundreds of sufferers. Although continually engaged in these good works he never neglected his family, devoting himself to his mother with the most tender and filial piety, being kind and considerate to his brothers and sisters, and most attentive to the wants of his servants and of every one in his household, with whom he had fixed hours of prayer in common and numerous other pious exercises.

The time arrived at last when he felt he must prepare his own family for martyrdom, and he was in fact, occupied in this very work when, before sunrise, the satellites appeared. Francis met them at the door. 'Whence come you, and why have you tarried so long? We have been impatiently waiting for you. Behold us! we are all ready. But it is not quite dawn, and you are tired, rest a little; take some food, and then we will all start with you in good order.' This reception filled the soldiers with amazement. They exclaimed, 'We have found Christians indeed!' The repast was served; Marie, the wife of Francis, herself prepared it for them; after which the satellites slept, whilst Francis exhorted his little band to bear courageously the trials and tortures which awaited them. Then they all assembled to the number of forty, and began their march. In front went the men with their elder boys, then followed the women with the younger children and the babies, and the satellites closed the procession. The journey, under the heat of a tropical sun, and accompanied as it was by the imprecations of the soldiers, was most painful and trying. Nevertheless the voice of Francis quelled all complaints, hushed the piteous cries of the children, and communicated to each the fortitude with which he himself was filled. 'Courage, brothers!' he cried; 'see the angel of God with a golden rod in his hand counting and measuring every step of your road! Look, and see, our Lord Jesus Christ with His Cross goes before you to Calvary!'

The very next day Francis was dragged before the judges, and ordered to apostatise.

'How!' he exclaimed; 'you wish me to perjure myself! If to be unfaithful to a human master is a crime, what would it be to be unfaithful towards God?' This intrepid answer so exasperated the mandarins that they caused his legs and arms to be broken, and tore his flesh in a thousand pieces. He received one hundred and ten strokes of the rotin; and it can only be attributed to an extraordinary grace that he did not die under the torture at that time. Then the judges produced one of the sacred books, and turning to Francis said, 'Read to us some pages of this book, that we may know what your religion is.' Francis joyfully consented, and read with such unction and fervour that the whole company rose to their feet with cries of admiration at the sublime lessons this Gospel contained. Nevertheless the heroic confessor was remanded to prison. For forty days, we are told, Francis suffered with invincible patience all the fearful tortures to which he was subjected, so that the executioners themselves surnamed him the *Rock*, on account of his apparent insensibility to pain. At last this venerable patriarch consummated his glorious martyrdom on the 12th September 1839.

His noble wife Mary, and her young family followed in his footsteps. Nothing was omitted to induce this intrepid woman to apostatise and save her little children from their sufferings. For a moment maternal love appeared to conquer her resolution. Her breast, torn by the pincers of the torturers, could no longer afford milk for her baby, whom all the while she had borne in her arms. With insidious speeches they tried to persuade her that by pronouncing some words with her lips she would satisfy the judges and save her child; but on understanding more fully what was implied by such an act, she hastened to her judges, retracting all she had said, saw her baby die of hunger, and then, with the rest of her family, marched courageously to the place of execution, and calmly presented her head to the sword of the executioner. Could anything in the annals of the Church be more heroic, or show more strongly the power of God's grace?

After the self-sacrifice of Mgr. Imbert, the persecution ceased by little and little; and in 1845 the new Bishop, Mgr. Férreol, under the guidance of Father Andrew Kim, effected an entrance into the Corea, accompanied by M. Daveluy.

The difficulties which the new Vicar-apostolic had to surmount were immense. With but two priests to help him, he had the spiritual needs of all the dispersed Christians in the Corea to attend to, many of whom were hiding in the most inaccessible parts of the peninsula. He could do nothing openly for the conversion of the heathen, as he was forced to keep himself rigorously concealed; nevertheless, what he was thus prevented from doing himself, the grace of God worked for him. Every year added to the multitude of adult conversions. The number of Christians, which the persecution had diminished to something like 7000, was doubled during the few years of his faithful administration of the diocese; and at the end of 1852 the Christians amounted to upwards of 11,000 souls.

The fatigues of so extraordinarily painful a mission, however, ruined the health of Mgr. Ferreol, and after a few months' illness he died on the 3d of February 1853; designating in his will Mgr. Berneux as his successor, subject to the approval of the Holy See.

The latter embarked at Shanghai the 7th January 1856, accompanied by two other missionaries, MM. Pourthié and Petitnicolas. The distance between this port and Corea is but small; in fair weather, four days is sufficient for the crossing; but with the difficulties arising from the inclemency of the season, and the necessity for concealment, their passage occupied two months, which was again prolonged by the ignorance of the pilot; and it was not until the 15th of March that they cast anchor opposite an extensive Corean village.

Here they were in Corea, but not as yet in the midst of their neophytes; the most difficult part of the undertaking had yet to be accomplished, viz. finding the vessel which was expected to meet them. 'M. Maistre,' writes Mgr. Berneux, 'who for eight years with heroic constancy had tried every point of the Corean frontier, and never once met the men who were to introduce him into the mission, had been obliged, after coming several times to this very spot, to return to China; and might not this be our own fate? For five days our bark visited every little creek of these islets, bearing a streamer with a large cross upon it, which was to be the signal to the Christians; but no one appeared. At length, towards nine in the morning of Good Friday, we perceived a small boat approaching us, the equipage of which replied to our signal by making the sign of the cross. After due recognition, they anchored at some little distance in order not to excite suspicion; yet, on account of the severe rain, it was not until Easter Sunday that we were able to quit the Chinese junk, and to go on board the Corean boat.

'After four days' sail in and out of the islands among the fishermen's boats, we were still fifteen leagues from the capital. Wind and water failing us, we at last got into a small boat with one courier and three rowers, and made for the land. We had adopted the mourning costume of the country for the purpose of concealment. At eleven in the evening the tide being against us, we determined to land and complete on foot the four or five leagues which remained. Confiding rather in the darkness of the night than in the broad borders of our straw hats, to cover our entrance into the town, we walked as quickly as the bad state of the roads and the kind of foot-gear we wore for the first time permitted, in order to arrive there before dawn. We reached the town in fact before sunrise; but as the king was absent, and the gates of the city for this reason could not be opened before daybreak, we took refuge in the house of a native Christian in order to make sure of a little rest. When the gates were opened, however, we made our entrance into this the first city of the kingdom. We walked in single file; I preceded by a Christian, and followed at a distance by M. Petitnicolas and M. Pourthié. I had a great wish to look at a grand mandarin who went out at that moment, surrounded by a numerous cortège; but I did not do so for fear of being recognised. The wind too, at that moment, threatened to carry away my protecting hat, whilst one of our party so avoided the use of his eyes, that he lost sight of us in the crowd; but was happily discovered again without much difficulty. A moment after we found ourselves under the roof of the excellent M. Daveluy, giving thanks to God for having so far prospered our voyage.'

CHAPTER XVII.

Short description of Corea. Corean race. Government. Classes. Dwellings. Customs in mourning. Food. Privations.

UNTIL the arrival of the French missionaries in 1835 little or nothing was known of the Corea.

It is true that a Dutch sailor, named Hamel, who was shipwrecked on this inhospitable coast in 1653, and afterwards escaped to Japan, published, on his return to Europe, a description of the country. But, with the lying habits of the natives, he was unable to arrive at any correct appreciation of the people or the kingdom; he could only relate what he himself saw and suffered during his thirteen years of slavery. We will proceed, therefore, to give a short description of the country and of the manners of its inhabitants.

The Corea forms a peninsula, bounded on the east by the sea of Japan, and on the west by the Yellow sea. In extent it may be compared to the kingdom of Italy. Intersected from north to south by a chain of mountains, Corea boasts of few plains, but is principally formed of rich valleys, irrigated by the numberless torrents which fall on all sides from the mountains above. Although situated in the same latitude as the south of Italy, the climate is extremely severe on account of its extensive forests and high mountains, many of which are covered with perpetual snow. Mgr. Imbert mentioned that in January the wine in the chalice froze during the celebration of the divine mysteries. The valleys of the Corea may be said to be nothing but great rice-fields. The ox is the only beast of burden; horses would be unable to live in the rice-fields, which are perpetually under water. The Corean himself is almost amphibious; all day long he works in the water. The fruits are the same in kind, but far inferior in flavour to those of France. Minerals abound: iron, copper, lead, and even gold and silver are found here: but no use is made of these riches. What copper they require is brought from Japan, and for domestic purposes it is used with a mixture of zinc.

Amongst the animals of the country the tiger is the most dreaded. Bears, boars, beavers, sable, and deer likewise abound. The forests are full of pheasants, but also of many dangerous kinds of snakes. The domestic animals are the horse, the ox, and the pig; the flesh of the latter is more delicate than our home pork: the Coreans rear likewise a quantity of fowls. The rivers are full of fish; and it is said that they contain crocodiles; but on this point the missionaries have said nothing.

The origin of the Coreans appears to be Tartar or Mongol. Yet their manners, customs, arts and sciences, are the same as the Chinese. They have the same religion, the same caligraphy, and the same language, only differently pronounced. The most remarkable feature of the country is its paucity of inhabitants. The Corean is of the ordinary height, with a round head, a little nose flattened between two fat cheeks, and generally with dark hair; very few have beards.

What strikes a Corean most in the physiognomy of a European is the prominence of his nose. When they speak of coming to pay the missionaries a visit, they say, 'They are going to see *the long nose of the Father.*' The Coreans are active and vigorous, fond of rest, but ready and willing to work when required; in summer, in fact, they work all day, and sleep but little: they are fond of music, and the villagers always possess some rude kind of instruments upon which they make a noise which is not inharmonious, and to which they sing and dance for a few minutes, and then return to their toil.

Although recognising, in a manner, the suzerainty of the Emperor of China, the King of Corea is, in reality, perfectly independent in the interior administration of his dominions. Two parties dispute the possession of power: these are the *Sipai*, or moderate, and the *Piokpai*, or violent party. The latter are the implacable enemies of the Christians, and it is when they are in power that the persecutions arise. But although the monarchy is absolute, the management of affairs is generally left to a few family favourites, who make use of their power in order to amass wealth. 'The oppressions under which the people groan in consequence,' writes Mgr. Berneux, ' have forced them into a state of chronic insurrection, not indeed against the king, whom they love, but against the mandarins, many of whom have been expelled, while the people revenged themselves by demolishing their houses.

'There are three classes amongst the Coreans — the nobles, the middle, and the lower class, among which latter slaves are to be found. The privileges of the nobles are very great. He may neither work nor employ himself in trade. He therefore lives on the people, who may refuse him nothing. His dwelling is sacred — even the mandarins dare not search it without great reflection, as, should there be no proofs of guilt attached to the noble, the mandarin and the agents of the police would suffer a severe penalty for their intrusion. Not a Corean but desires most ardently this title to nobility.

'I myself,' continues Mgr. Berneux, 'have adopted this dignity, as by this means I can pass rivers and lodge in inns without danger of discovery. But, as I should have been obliged to wait too long before I could obtain from government the letters of nobility, I have given them to myself. I have adopted all the manners of a noble, excepting the blows and the exactions. I have purchased a house in the capital, and have taken a Christian, a true noble, and installed him in the outer apartment. His wife and children occupy one of the interior rooms, and I lodge in the other. This family appears to the world to be proprietor of the house, and no one dreams that a European Bishop resides therein. But if the nobles have their privileges, the women hawkers and beggars have theirs. These women are permitted to enter, unannounced, into the inner court; and as my red beard, my eyes, and fair complexion belie any idea of my being of Corean blood, I am obliged to remain shut up in my little room from morning till night, and from night till morning, without the liberty of going out into the court, without opening my window, even in summer, and without speaking above a whisper.

'This little room is in fact my entire palace. Here morning after morning, upon a chest which serves as an altar, I celebrate holy Mass; here, seated upon the ground, I work; here also I take my two meals, and receive the catechists by means of whom I communicate with the Christians; for, except the four catechists, and a few others who are necessary to me, no one amongst the Christians is allowed to come and see me. My house is not supposed even to be known to them, and they may not reveal it to others when it chances to become known to any. Notwithstanding all these precautions, however, my house is often suspected, and in this way I have lost two of considerable value, and two others I have been unable to sell.

'The Corea is divided into eight provinces, which are again subdivided. The chief town is the only one of any importance, and here alone can be found in any degree the conveniences of life. It is situated in the midst of mountains, and enclosed by thick high walls, with a large population, but ill-constructed. With few exceptions, the streets are narrow and winding; the houses low and miserable; the rooms are very small; and tables, beds, and chairs are unknown. Seated cross-legged, tailor-fashion, from the king to the peasant, the Corean sits, works, and talks; he knows no more convenient posture; and you would find me squatted in the same fashion if you could pay me a visit in the Corea.

'The houses, though small, are clean; they are warmed from beneath, and the floors are covered with a kind of oil-paper, which is carefully wiped every morning. This cleanliness is particularly necessary, since the Corean, in his robe of white linen, sits upon it from morning till evening. Glass being unknown, paper alone fills our window-panes.'

One peculiar feature of Corean costume is their mourning, which consists of a coarse dress of unbleached linen, and an immense osier hat which covers the whole head down to the shoulders. A man in mourning is as one dead; he sees no one, he hardly looks up to the sky. If he goes out, his face is veiled; if interrogated, he may decline to reply. To kill any kind of animal when one is in mourning is a crime. Whilst travelling they keep aloof from every one, and at the inns on the road they require a separate room, and refuse communication with every one. This custom was favourable for the missionaries, who put themselves into mourning without any scruple.

With regard to the food, the ruined condition of the Christians had reduced them to such extreme poverty, that they had great difficulty in procuring such of the necessaries of life as fell to the share of the poor. 'The poor people,' writes Mgr. Berneux, 'live on wretched food; a little rice boiled in water, with a turnip or a few cabbage-leaves chopped up raw, and seasoned with salt and pimento, constitutes the whole of their nourishment from one end of the year to the other; happy is he indeed who never lacks these!' and the missionaries fared no better.

Nevertheless, after every account of privation or suffering, which it was his lot to endure, Mgr. Berneux never failed to reassure his friends by the evidence he unconsciously gave of the supernatural graces with which he was so richly endowed. 'Do not be unhappy,' he writes in a letter to M. Henri de la Bouillerie, 'at the thought of what we have to endure. All these privations are so abundantly made up for, that we reckon them as nothing. The faith and fervour of our neophytes compensate for all, and the zeal with which they work at the conversion of their pagan friends, and their heroic constancy under suffering, is as edifying as it is consoling.' He adds: 'We have besides resources that you little suspect. Remember the three or four leagues, which the missionary often has to make on foot before breakfast, then the eight or nine hours spent in catechising or confessing; all this gives to our rice and water, salt fish, and vegetable leaves, a flavour which a diplomatist himself would appreciate?' Is it possible to admire enough the wonderful grace which gave strength to bear and courage to endure such terrible privations, not for a day or a week, but for every moment of every day, even till time should be no more for them! Could it be endured for any thing less grand than the glory of God and the salvation of souls?

There is one more custom among the Coreans deserving of notice, and that is, the observance of the Hoan-Kap or sixtieth anniversary of their birth, which they celebrate with every description of rejoicing. The poorest people will starve half the year rather than not provide a sufficiently gorgeous feast on this occasion. But when this anniversary occurs to any member of the royal family the tax upon every member of society is oppressive in the highest degree, as, if the presents offered are not sufficient, the whole province falls into disgrace, and the governor in all probability loses his head.

CHAPTER XVIII.

Mgr. Berneux fixes his residence in the capital. Method of administration. Great precautions. Interesting details. Faith and fervour of the Christians: their heroism and power of endurance. Consecration of M. Daveluy as co-adjutor Bishop of Acônes.

It was in May 1856 that Mgr. Berneux effected his entrance into the Corea. He profited by the summer months to make himself master of the Corean language, which in many respects resembles the Chinese; and, although still in very bad health, he started in the month of November following in order to visit the Christians in the other provinces. He had reserved to himself the capital where they were most numerous and sixty neighbouring villages.

'The capital,' he writes, 'we divide into four quarters, and at the head of each we have a catechist. It is through them that the Christians communicate with me, and they accompany me on my visits to the sick.

'Twice a year, in spring and in autumn, when I begin the administration, the catechists seek among the Christians a place which may serve as a chapel. This it is always very difficult to find. In the poor dwellings of our Christians it is often impossible to stand upright for the celebration of holy Mass, or to locate the five-and-twenty persons whom I ought to confess. Those which are not so inconvenient are either in a dangerous quarter, or the family is not all Christian. But, in order that our meetings should remain secret, it would be necessary for us to have about forty houses amongst which the Christians of the capital might be divided; but I have not even fifteen.

'When the Christians have prepared everything, I go before daybreak to the house where I am to administer the sacraments. Twenty-five Christians are in waiting; the men in the court, the women in one of the two small rooms of the house; the other, converted into a chapel, is for me.

'After a few words with our dear neophytes, who are always overjoyed to see their Bishop and to receive the sacraments, for which they are really famishing, I recite my office, and during this time the catechist takes down the names of all who are coming to confession, with all the circumstances concerning them which may be useful for me to know. After this some books are read by way of meditation, in order to prepare them for the reception of the sacraments.

'After breakfast follows catechism and examination in Christian doctrine, then confessions, during which time the women attend, in their apartment, to the spiritual readings. In the evening the catechumens are examined; and then I go to rest, weary but content with my day's work; unless, indeed, some wife, unknown to her pagan husband, comes at midnight for instruction. In these cases, even a timid noble lady, who has never before crossed the threshold of her own door, finds courage when it is a question of receiving the sacraments. Disguised as a poor woman she comes when all her family are asleep, in the middle of the night, to the house where the Christians are assembled. The number of these ladies is considerable; and although in the midst of a pagan family, they find means to fulfil their duties most exactly. In the middle of the night they come to confession, and assist at the three-o'clock Mass, after which they reënter their homes, as they left them, without being suspected either by husband or family. Woe to them if their nocturnal absence were discovered by their husbands! Instant death by poison would be the punishment of their temerity.

'After Mass follows the baptism of children and adults, confirmations, and occasionally extreme unction. The Christians return to their respective homes often weeping with joy: whilst the missionary hastens, thankfully, to the next house to repeat the exercises and the functions of the previous day. The number of Christians in this town is over 1400. The administration, therefore, of this town in this secret manner requires no less than two months.'

In another letter, Mgr. Berneux adds:

'It is tiring enough sometimes to drive one distracted; more than once it has happened to me that I have fallen fast asleep in the middle of my room, to awake in the morning with one sock in my hand, and the other on my foot.

'There are fewer difficulties to contend with in

the country, where the Christians have taken refuge among the mountains, forming little hamlets, containing five or six families each. Although the journeys on foot are extremely fatiguing, passing from one village to another, yet it is possible for the missionary to breathe freely and to take sufficient sleep. Here he is able to spend several days amongst these simple creatures, who receive him with every mark of devotion and respect. It is not rare to find amongst them families who have once been opulent and who have enjoyed the highest dignities of the state, but have given up all for their faith. Here they would be able to live, though poor, if it were not for the continually renewed persecutions; but the cupidity of the satellites and other enemies of the faith finds them out even in their rocky retreats; and from time to time these poor but faithful people are suddenly invaded, robbed, and chased from their humble homes. This, what I may call private persecution, unrepressed by the mandarins, is even more disastrous than the more sanguinary ones carried on by the government. They form besides a more effectual barrier to conversions, and fill the hearts of our neophytes with despair.'

'We work on,' again writes Mgr. Berneux, 'with all our strength, but with the greatest precaution. The axe is ever hanging over our heads, and the least accident might cause a fearful persecution. You may understand how, in this position, we can have neither chapels nor regular places of resort for our Christians. On Sunday from twelve to fifteen assemble, sometimes in one house, sometimes in another; and always most secretly. They recite together in an undertone the prayers ordered by the Bishop, and hear the gospel for the day explained. The rest of the day is occupied in saying the rosary, in learning the catechism, and teaching it to the children; and this is all that our Coreans can do towards the sanctification of Sunday! Were it permitted them to assist at Mass, all would be lost, and I should be certain of being captured before the end of a month.'

M. l'Abbé Féron gives a most interesting picture of the spiritual state of his flock, in answer to a question which very naturally suggests itself, as to how, with so few spiritual helps, the Corean is enabled to live in a state of grace. 'Truly,' he writes, 'our poor Christians are very much neglected. I alone have the care of the administration of more than 3500 souls, dispersed over ninety different villages; and in order to visit them, I am obliged to travel over nearly 400 leagues during the winter, amongst mountains all but impassable, and often covered with snow. Consequently our Christians see the priest but once a year, assist at Mass but once, hear the word of God but once, confess once, communicate once, and very few ever receive the Sacraments at the hour of death. Nevertheless we have every hope that the largest number of them will be saved, for the grace of God marvellously supplies our deficiencies. This is certain: that in spite of the absence of spiritual aids, in spite of the bad examples with which they are surrounded, and although it cannot be denied that some of them fall occasionally into very grave sins, still it is quite

K

certain that a very great number live from year to year without committing a single mortal sin. I believe I do not exaggerate when I affirm that it is by no means rare to meet with those who have preserved their baptismal innocence until the day of their death. It is true that we do not find amongst them that gentle tender piety which accompanies a frequent reception of the Sacraments, and the continual Presence of our Lord in the midst of us; but to make up for this, God has granted to them an extraordinary spirit of faith, and a most profound horror of the superstitions of their country, together with great fidelity to their religious exercises, a lively devotion to our Blessed Mother, and an ardent desire for the Sacraments. Thus it is rare that any one fails in his morning or evening devotions, his daily rosary, and in the celebration of feasts, even those of devotion. And although we tell them each time that the omission of such feasts and of the daily chaplet is not a sin, still they none the less continue to accuse themselves when it has happened. We have accustomed them also to the practice of saluting each other, whenever it is possible, by the ejaculation, "Praised be Jesus Christ!" We endeavour to inspire them with a horror of gambling and of drunkenness, and we punish severely in cases of necessity. God blesses our labours, and all goes well. The people are trained to obedience; and though there may be occasional trouble, it is not difficult to guide them; for their affection and gratitude to the missionaries know no bounds.'

'Amongst our Christians,' writes Mgr. Berneux,

'there are many who belong to families who have no idea that such is the case—women who have been baptised unknown to their husbands, children unknown to their parents, &c. The difficulties they have to overcome in the practice of their religion in these cases are innumerable; nevertheless faith makes them very ingenious. They continue to avoid detection, and to recite their daily prayers morning and evening; and, what is more difficult still, to keep clear of joining in the superstitions of their country, and to leave their homes yearly for confession in the catacombs, where we are often obliged to conceal ourselves. Were it found out that they are Christians, their bodies might be broken with blows, but their constancy would be unshaken.'

'The Corean character,' he continues, 'has an energy which I have met with nowhere else. In 1839 we had children of twelve and fourteen years of age who, being dragged before the mandarins, have borne having their legs broken, to be flogged nearly to death, and afterwards to be decapitated, without apostatising. I have with me now a young Christian, converted by his mother, who has but just given a proof of his inflexible constancy. On hearing of his conversion, his uncles went to him, imploring him to spare his family the ignominy attached to the Christian name. Caresses, menaces, and at length blows were resorted to. "Strike," said he; "kill me if you will. I have become a Christian in order to save my soul; your blows are a ladder which will lead me to heaven; the death you prepare for me will open its doors at once." They threatened to take him to the mandarin. "Very well, I will follow you; but what can the mandarin do to me? Kill me? Then will he send me to heaven. Will he exile me? God is everywhere, and everywhere I shall serve Him." Tired out at last by his constancy, his relations left him in peace; and this man has brought to me for baptism eleven pagans, converted and instructed by himself.

'A young pagan woman, whose mother had succeeded in converting her, was occupied secretly in learning the catechism. The book fell into her husband's hand, who burned it without speaking. She procured another, which, when he found, he vented the most fearful imprecations against her and against the Christian religion. Without disturbing herself, she replied that, being his wife, he was at liberty to curse her, to beat her, and even to repudiate her; that she was quite prepared for this, and for everything else; but that if he thought to prevent her embracing the Christian religion, he would never succeed. Thereupon she laid herself quietly down, in order to receive his blows. The infuriated husband beat her without mercy; and after covering her with blood, she rose, and pointing to her wounds, she said to him, "You may do this again and again; but I shall be a Christian." In truth, she came but a few days after, and received baptism.

'The Corean possesses the most perfect dispositions for receiving the faith. Once convinced, he accepts and attaches himself to it, in spite of all sacrifices it may cost him. I have with me at the present moment a young man of family, whom I shall baptise in a month's time. Besides his legitimate wife, he had a concubine, whom, in spite of the remonstrances of his family, he persevered in keeping. He hears of our religion; he reads our books, and is converted. At once he renounces the dignities of his birth, and sets himself to study the prayers and the catechism. We tell him that religion will not permit him to have a concubine; and the same day he sends her away. His old uncle, a mandarin of the capital, who had so vainly exhorted him to separate himself from this woman, being witness of the facility with which the youth broke away from this tie which had so long enthralled him, desired to know the cause. It is not hidden from him; in consequence of which, after having studied our books, this old man sells his mule of office and his house, throws up his charge, and begins himself to learn the catechism.'

Another marvellous instance is thus related:

'An old septuagenarian heard of the Christian religion, and by chance met with a book of ours. He read, and was convinced. But as the post he occupied in Corea was an important one, and incompatible with the duties of Christianity, he gave it up, and retired into private life. His peculiar circumstances, however, with regard to his family exposed him to offend God; and so to avoid this he feigned imbecility, neither washing himself nor speaking to any one. For several years he has thus been able to fulfil all the duties of a faithful Catholic, without its being possible for him to receive the grace of baptism. His sons, suspecting his inten-

tions, have taken good care that no stranger should
come near the old man, knowing well that in the
event of his becoming a Christian they would run
the risk of losing all their employments. However,
I have succeeded at last, and a catechist is gone to
him, who, I trust, will succeed in baptising him.'
This hope, he afterwards tells us, was fulfilled.

'Of such traits I could enumerate thousands,'
continues he. 'O, how you would love my Coreans!
how you would pray for us! God has surely great
designs for this mission, judging by the graces He
grants to it, and the expedients He suggests to souls
naturally so simple and timid.'

The heroism of the Christians was the greatest
recompense and the sweetest consolation to the missionaries in the midst of their sufferings. On this
subject Mgr. Berneux wrote in July 1857:

'Thanks be to God, we have not at present any
general persecution, and we are able to administer
our Christians in comparative peace. The only thing
is that we are obliged to take excessive precautions
against our presence in the kingdom becoming suspected. Thus we are exposed to many and great
privations and sufferings. But it is the life of the
missionary—suffer, suffer more, suffer always. But
these sufferings, these privations, I would not exchange them for all the world has to give. O, how
well God knows how to make up for all that is endured for His sake! When I see the fervour of our
Christians; when I look upon this mass of pagans
coming to me and seeking baptism, although in doing

so they abandon all dignities, wealth, family ties, and expose themselves to certain death, I weep for joy, and I would willingly suffer a thousandfold more.' 'I have never been so poor, or so deprived of earthly comforts as now,' he writes again; 'but never have I been so happy!'

Upon the arrival of Mgr. Berneux in the Corea, the Christians enjoyed comparative peace : the presence of several French men-of-war upon the seas between Corea and China disquieted the government. 'The year 1857,' wrote the Vicar-apostolic, 'has been a year specially blessed, for which we cannot sufficiently thank God. No persecution has arisen to try us. I have taken advantage of the tranquillity we are permitted to enjoy, in order to summon all our missionaries to the capital, for the purpose of assisting in the consecration of my coadjutor. It is the first time that such a ceremony has taken place in Corea. Our Christians would gladly have taken part in it; but prudence did not permit us to admit any one. It was therefore with closed doors, and in the middle of the night, that M. Daveluy, who for eleven years has rendered such important service to this mission, received episcopal consecration under the title of Bishop of Acônes. We were still assembled, after a synod of three days, when, on the 31st of March, we were joined by a *confrère* whom no one was expecting, M. l'Abbé Féron. Thus this mission of Corea, formerly so inaccessible to Europeans, which but two years ago had no Bishop, and whose administration was entirely in the hands of two missionaries and a native priest, has now two Bishops, four foreign apostles, and one native priest.'*

* These missionaries were MM. Maistre, Pourthié, Petit-nicolas, Féron, and the Corean priest Thomas Tschoez. M. Maistre arrived in the Corea in 1852, and died on the 20th December 1857, assisted in his last moments by Mgr. Berneux.

CHAPTER XIX.

Difficulties of missionary work. Printing. Baptism of infants in danger of death. Work of the 'Holy Infancy.' Native clergy. Foundation of two colleges: the movement begins to be general: hopes brighten. Fresh persecutions in 1860. Cholera and famine. Two printing-presses are set up. Slow but gradual development of the mission.

ALL missionary work amongst the heathen is accompanied by the greatest difficulties; and the Corea is no exception. The faithful, being so much mixed up with the heathen, are exposed to the temptation of taking part in the superstitious practices surrounding them. Polygamy is frequent, and usury habitual and excessive. It was therefore necessary to adopt a uniform rule for the conduct of the Christians, and for that of the heathen desirous of baptism, in order to fit them for the fearful trials which would probably await them. It was found necessary to instruct the converts completely in all the mysteries of the faith before admitting them to the Sacrament of baptism; in consequence of which, although the number of adult baptisms for some time was on the decrease, that of the catechumens was always increasing. 'For the last two or three years,' writes Mgr. Berneux, 'the number of adult baptisms has been a little on the decrease: in 1861 it amounted to 751, and last year it was 686; but we have now more than 1300 catechumens.' In the instruction of the Christians. Mgr. Daveluy and Father Tschoey, and some others, had written elementary works, or translated some of the best European works of devotion into the Corean dialect. A printing-press was set up in order to facilitate the multiplication of these necessary books. The last persecution has unhappily led to the destruction of the printing-press, and to the loss of many books, which were found in the houses of the Christians.

The faithful showed the greatest zeal for the baptism of infant heathens in danger of death. Every year in this way many thousands of these innocent creatures were thus regenerated. Mgr. Berneux founded amongst them the work of the Holy Infancy, but not with such great results as in the Chinese missions. In China it is very common to find children exposed. In the Corea, on the contrary, such exposition is rare. Moreover, as etiquette forbids the entrance of men into the women's apartments, the baptism of children dangerously sick is a very difficult task. However, every year from eight to ten thousand children were baptised, who passed soon after to the happiness of heaven. About fifty, rescued from the public streets, were brought up by the Church.

'The necessity in which we are placed,' writes Mgr. Berneux in November 1862, 'to avoid the suspicion of the heathen, does not allow us to have schools for girls, because the Coreans do not have them. We have a few for boys; and it is with great difficulty we keep them. The heathen of the neighbourhood often ask that their little ones may be admitted. If we consent, or if we refuse, the trouble is equally great. We are often, therefore, obliged to leave the care of instruction to the parents.'

The chief work which Mgr. Berneux proposed to accomplish was the formation of a native clergy. He appealed to the devotion of MM. Pourthié and Petitnicolas to give up the active ministry, for which they had a great vocation; and committed to their care two little colleges, hidden amongst the mountains, in which he placed a few young men, the dearest hope of the Corean mission. In 1863 he writes, 'I have actually seven missionaries, who work vigorously. I hope to receive an eighth, with two pupils who come from our general college, when they have completed their theological course. In my internal seminary, I have three students of philosophy—three sixth-form and five new pupils who are learning the Chinese character, the knowledge of which is indispensable to this mission.'

It does not appear that the Corean priests ordained by Mgr. Berneux were arrested and put to death in the last persecution: it is therefore to be hoped that they have been spared to watch over the poor Christians whilst awaiting the new European missionaries, who will doubtless soon take the places of Mgr. Berneux and his glorious companions in martyrdom.

Although there was no actual general persecution for many years, Mgr. Berneux writes, in 1858, that the Christians were constantly harassed by local vexations; but now the case became different. 'In the course of the winter, in various parts of the kingdom, Christians were seized and imprisoned. In the district of Mgr. d'Acônes a whole village fled into the mountains, to avoid the pursuit of the satellites. It appeared as though the persecution was about to become general, when all at once the prisoners were set free, the fugitives came down from the mountains, and Mgr. the Coadjutor, who had also taken flight, returned to his retreat. The captives were released, whilst one of their accusers, who had presented himself to the mandarin with a list of one hundred Christian heads of families, was garrotted, thrown into prison, and beaten to death. The issue of this affair is a victory for us; an important one too, so far as it gives courage to our neophytes, and reassures those of the heathen whom fear keeps back.'

'We have all remarked,' he continues, 'the movement which is being felt in the whole vicariate. In the capital, above all, this appears to be the case. Unheard-of efforts are made to obtain instruction; the fervour of the Christians gains the heathen. One of the most noble families of the kingdom has embraced the faith: the head of this house, a near connection of the reigning king, has been baptised this winter. Many others will follow this example: eight new stations have been formed in the district of the Rev. F. Tschoey; and seven others will be opened next year.'

In 1860, however, fresh vexations began to try

the Christians. Mgr. Berneux writes in October to M. Nouard: 'Last year, had I written to you, my communications would have been full of joy and hope. I had but one anxiety, that of being insufficient for the work. But now our position is altogether changed. For ten months the missionary has been obliged to keep to his retreat; our books have been burned; our neophytes dispersed or thrown into prison; their goods pillaged, their villages burned; and our catechumens, my joy and my crown, probably for the most part discouraged. And this is the state of my mission; arising from no order of the government, but through the head of the police, in order to enrich his relations with the spoils of the Christians. In such cases the shepherd ought to be where the sheep suffer most; but the vigilance of the heathen obliges us to keep in our retreats, in order not to bring fresh calamities upon our unhappy flocks. We can but suffer and pray, while we adore the designs of Almighty God.'

In another letter he says: 'A persecution of eight months has ruined all my hopes. More than fifty Christians have been cast into prison; upwards of 200 families have been driven from their homes, which have been reduced to ashes; and since all they possessed has been taken from them, nothing remains for these poor Christians—without money, without clothes, and without roofs—but to die of hunger.'

The venerable prelate says farther, in another letter: 'During the eight days, or rather the eight nights, that I wandered in search of a shelter, I met some of these families in their flight. I know no spectacle more heartrending than that of these poor women walking with difficulty across the thick snow, leading by the hand the little children who could walk, and carrying upon their backs or in their arms those of a more tender age. O, truly it needed great grace not to hate those who, in order to enrich themselves with a few thousand francs, could thus make gain of the sufferings of so many, whose only crime is to be Christians. The government, however, has refrained as yet from putting our Christians to death. Thirty have been released; but ten are still in prison, where they will, I fear, die of hunger. One, an aged woman, expired in the midst of the tortures inflicted upon her, sooner than renounce her faith. By the sanctity of her life, and her zeal for the conversion of her pagan neighbours, she had succeeded in gaining many souls for our dear Lord; and He has rewarded her with the grace of martyrdom.

'But notwithstanding all these miseries, our Christians serve God as before, and many pagans are hereby converted. They perfectly understand that the thing of importance here below is to save one's soul, and that all is useless to him who is damned. Would to God that people at home would understand it as well! It is indeed a source of deep grief to me to think of the number of so-called Christians in France, who live as if they had never heard of God, notwithstanding all the spiritual treasures in their possession; whilst here, where our Christians see their priest but one day in the year, and where they cannot practise their religion except by exposing themselves to poverty, torture, and death—here, I say, we have very few tepid Christians.

'Notwithstanding the search that has been made for us all through this persecution, neither I nor my missionaries have been taken. I have merely lost a few thousand francs, upon which, however, we depended for existence during the next year. But God for whom we are working will take charge of our wants. There is no need for anxiety on this account.'

But vengeance was also in the hand of God. In 1860 He sent the cholera, whose ravages were felt throughout the whole kingdom. More than 40,000 persons were carried off; while of these, it is worthy of remark, only thirty Christians fell victims to the fearful scourge. After this, in consequence of the excessive rains, a famine broke out, in the train of which followed those bands of thieves whom no one attempted to repress, and who fell upon and ravaged entire villages.

These troubles arrested for a time the pursuit of the Christians. Moreover a few months later arrived, like a thunderclap, the news of the capture of Pekin, and the peace imposed upon China, the terms of which included liberty of religion. The rich inhabitants of Corea, fearing an attack of the French, fled to the mountains with their treasures; and, indeed, had a few French men-of-war appeared at that moment before the capital, no doubt terms would have been obtained which would have released the Christians from their troubles. But the time went by;

and when later on a pacific intervention was attempted, so far from the happy results which Mgr. Berneux anticipated, the evils which he dreaded were simply hastened.

Thus, though the mission continued slowly to develop itself, the hatred of the heathen carried on a constant and cruel persecution against the Christians in all the provinces; and, on the other hand, in spite of this ever-increasing persecution, religion stirred up the people in as irresistible a manner as it was secret and slow. 'We do not lose courage,' says Mgr. Berneux in 1863. 'Such faith as lives in the hearts of our Christians will touch the heart of God. Better days will come. The seed which we sow in tears will produce a hundredfold, to the glory of God and to the confusion of the devil.

'Notwithstanding all difficulties, we work as though we were in peace. Already we reckon nine Europeans, occupied all the year round in the cultivation of this little vineyard. A tenth is coming, with two students who have completed their theology at our seminary of Pinang. Thus reinforced, we may be enabled to visit our Christians twice a year. Fervour increases with instruction, and with fervour and instruction the number of conversions is doubled.

'Thanks be to God, we have at great peril succeeded in establishing two printing-presses, which have done duty for two years: we are, therefore, well supplied with books. These printing-presses are everything to us. One province, where we had not as yet planted our standard, has given itself to us entirely, and at once. Above twenty men have come above sixty leagues to ask for baptism at the capital. By their example, more than 200 have abjured their idols, and are learning the catechism. It is probable that in April I shall send M. l'Abbé Féron to baptise those who are instructed, and organise the station.'

Thus from year to year we may follow the holy missionary in his apostolic labours, and take part in his sorrows and his joys. There was no year without some letter from him, which is marvellous, considering the extreme difficulty of communications at this time with the Corea.

'In order to send a letter,' writes M. l'Abbé Féron, 'it must pass by Mandchouria, hid in a courier's boot. This courier has to do 200 leagues on foot in the depth of winter, under pretext of buying goods at the annual fair which is held on the frontiers. He gives our letters to the messenger sent by Mgr. Verolles, who in return brings us back anything we may have come from Europe rolled up in Chinese goods. But Mgr. Berneux remained for three or four years without any tidings whatever of his family or friends, in consequence of the loss of several of these packets; and this privation was one which he felt most keenly, although he reproached himself for being saddened by it, and says he is "like a baby" for caring so much for his old home, and fears he is not yet sufficiently "detached."'

But we must hurry to a conclusion. It is not difficult to perceive that such labours and such successes were the work of no ordinary man; but the character and peculiar graces of Mgr. Berneux ought to occupy a separate chapter.

We will only add that his love and respect for the Holy See were those of a tender and devoted son to his father; and, on his side, the Sovereign Pontiff appreciated fully the virtues of the holy prelate, and never omitted to write a few encouraging words to him and his generous Corean flock. When the letters from Rome arrived, Mgr. Berneux would exclaim with joy: 'See how tenderly our little mission is loved by the Sovereign Pontiff! Every year, in spite of our unworthiness, he sends us a few lines of congratulation and blessing, signed with his very own hand. What an encouragement this is to our work, and what a cause of thankfulness to Almighty God!'

CHAPTER XX.

Character of Mgr. Berneux. His extraordinary activity and self-denial. His tenderness and care of his missionaries. Their unbounded love and respect.

THE great characteristics of Mgr. Berneux may be summed up as follows: the greatest generosity in the service of God; a complete abandonment of himself to His adorable will; extraordinary patience, entire detachment, and profound humility.

The Apostle St. Paul has said that it is well for us to plant and to water, but that to God alone belongs the increase. Mgr. Berneux not only understood, but acted upon this great truth. In every letter of his we find him seeking the prayers of others for his own sanctification, in order to the more perfect success of his mission. Notwithstanding his constant and arduous labours, we are told by M. Calais, a Corean missionary, that he devoted a considerable time to prayer. He had a most tender devotion towards the Blessed Virgin, and constantly recommended the same fidelity to his missionaries. He seldom failed to recite the whole rosary; and when in residence in the capital he never omitted the exercises of the month of Mary. He consecrated to the Mother of God his entire mission, and placed each division under the patronage of one of her feasts. 'To this deep piety,' M. Calais continues, ' our venerable Vicar-apostolic united a rare capacity for the administration of his flock. His great activity left him no rest, and he himself did the work of half-a-dozen ordinary men. . . . . Under his direction, the Corean mission made wonderful progress; and the discipline and instruction of the Christians became every year more and more admirable. Whenever he met a Christian, no matter what might be his age or condition, his first questions were: Do you pray aright? Have you learned the catechism?'

From M. l'Abbé Féron we learn, that all this work was accomplished in spite of great suffering from bad health, aggravated, no doubt, by poor and insufficient diet. It was not uncommon for him to work twenty hours out of the twenty-four, and then to begrudge himself the four hours left for sleep.

Again we learn that his patience and strength of mind in the midst of these sufferings and privation were inexhaustible. The heat of summer aggravated his bodily sufferings, confined as he was at that time of year altogether to his little room, where he could not speak above a whisper, and was obliged to be careful how he made the smallest movement: when advised to remove into the country, in order to enjoy greater freedom, he would always reply that the general should ever occupy the most difficult post.

By the accounts of the persecution which broke out in the Corea towards the end of the year 1860, we learn something of the anxiety and moral pains which he had to endure, to say nothing of his physical sufferings. Mgr. Berneux at the time was on one of his visitations in that unhappy district, and only escaped falling into the hands of the satellites by passing eight days and eight nights on mountains covered with snow, and infested by tigers. He arrived at his house in the capital but just in time to save the little property of the mission, which would otherwise have fallen into the hands of the persecutors, by the timidity of those left in charge. The uncertainty respecting the fate of his coadjutor and the other missionaries, of whom he had received no news, pressed also grievously upon his health. Although he rallied, he never entirely recovered from this shock. His hair became gray, and his beard perfectly white.

But in spite of these multiplied fatigues, which, as we have seen, reduced him frequently to a state of extreme weakness, Mgr. Berneux never took advantage of any dispensations. His food, when alone, consisted of rice cooked with water, and some salt vegetables. Meat, fish, and even eggs, rarely appeared on his table. Latterly he even denied himself the use of rice-wine.

But though so severe with himself, he was full of care and kindness towards his missionaries, desiring them to make use of every possible relaxation when overwhelmed with work. When they visited him, he endeavoured as much as possible to make up to them for the privations which every one suffers in the Corea. Thus, he who never tasted bread when alone (for it is not made in Corea) would grind the corn with his own hands, and make some bread himself, that he might have the pleasure of offering it to the missionaries when they came to see him; and he would put some into their bag at parting, and send little presents of it to his brethren at a distance.

'In spite of his multifarious occupations,' writes M. Calais, 'Mgr. Berneux was never too busy to attend to the wants or wishes of his missionaries.' They wrote to him continually, and his answers were not only prompt but admirably clear on every difficult point. His letters are models of theological knowledge, experience, and wisdom. It was a real treat to any of the missionaries to be able to spend a few days with him; and they always returned to their labours with fresh heart, fresh courage, and minds thoroughly at rest. One of them wrote on a certain occasion: 'I envy you your happiness at being with our much-loved Bishop. I am sure you will do your best to profit by the time you are permitted to spend with him; for they are precious moments, of which we shall never know the full value till he is taken from us.'

Do not these little details reveal the tenderness of a mother for her children? There was, indeed, amongst the missionaries but one heart and one feeling, and that was the respectful love and devotion of children towards one who was as a father and mother to them all.

Mgr. Daveluy gives the same evidence: 'Our mission is flourishing; our missionaries are happy;

there is life and vigour in all our works; and every one is satisfied, in spite of difficulties and privations. But how could the result be otherwise with such a Bishop? His generous zeal communicates itself to every one. In spite of his age, his physical sufferings, which are continual, and his excess of work, he is really the soul of the whole mission, giving an impulse to everything and multiplying himself with a zeal and an ardour which keeps up the feeling of generous emulation amongst us all. Pray to God,' he adds, ' that He may preserve to us our saint-like head, for he alone is capable of maintaining things on a good footing, and his love for souls would move mountains.'

CHAPTER XXI

Death of the king in 1864. Change affects the prospects of the mission. Presence of missionaries known to the authorities. Last letter of Mgr. Berneux to his friends. Demand of Russia for a concession of territory. The Bishops are called upon to mediate. Their mediation subsequently refused. Arrest, trial, and death of the missionaries. Conclusion.

IN the year 1864, the king of Corea died: leaving no children to inherit his throne, the regal power devolved upon a woman, the widow of a previous king. This woman adopted a child, the son of a Corean prince, and placed the government in the hands of his father.

This change of monarchs, which produced likewise a change of ministers, was the beginning of the great disasters which followed for the Corean church. Petitions were presented to government, demanding the restoration of all ancient customs, and the entire destruction of the Christian religion. Reports of the most alarming kind were spread, and terror not unnaturally took possession of the whole mission.

The presence of European missionaries, and especially that of the Vicar-apostolic, had at length become known to the authorities. From the year 1863 their mourning costume had ceased to be any protection. On one occasion, when visiting some new stations, Mgr. Berneux was even seized and beaten by the pagans; but he was released. It was not as yet considered safe to do anything with him.

The year 1865 passed in alternations of hope and fear. The health of Monseigneur was fast giving way; and he describes himself as an old white-headed, white-bearded man, whom his own friends would not recognise. He was now also unable to make the long journeys on foot which he had been accustomed to do. Nevertheless he and his missionaries continued to work day and night without ceasing, and their labours were rewarded by the continued and increasing fervour of the Christians. 'Our fatigues,' he writes to his sister, 'are great; but our consolations are greater. My days are passed in instructing and confessing good Christians, and in confirming and baptising the converted heathen. In three weeks I have travelled over 150 leagues across the mountains, and I have baptised 140 converts.

'Last spring the government thought to have exterminated us; but God has not judged me worthy of martyrdom, and He has had pity on this little flock. The persecution has not openly broken out, and here we are still. I recommend my mission to your prayers, and to the prayers of the faithful at Château-du-Loir. Tell every one you meet that your brother, who for five-and-twenty years has been an exile from France, prays continually for his native town, and that he asks in return a daily "Ave Maria" for the conversion of the Corea.'

This letter, the last probably that Mgr. Berneux

wrote home, concludes by the most affectionate words, addressed to his family and friends. He felt that he was saying farewell; that his strength was exhausted, and that he should soon be permitted to enjoy the rest which God had prepared for him. But the counsel of the Almighty had provided for him a greater honour still. That glorious crown, which he so nearly attained at the opening of his missionary career, was now about to be granted to him, as the worthy recompense of the sufferings and fatigues of an apostolate of five-and-twenty years, and as the seal of the doctrine he had preached. As St. Leo so beautifully expresses it: 'For the teaching of God's people, no way is more efficacious than that of martyrdom. Eloquence may carry away our hearers; or reason bring about conviction; but examples are worth more than words; and more perfect is it to teach by works than by words.' 'Ad erudiendum Dei populum, nullorum est utilior forma quam martyrum. Sit eloquentia facilis ad exhortandum, sit ratio efficax ad suadendum; validiora tamen sunt exempla quam verba, et plenius est opere docere quam voce.' *Serm.* LXXXIII. *in festo S. Laurentii.*

The account which follows, and which is drawn from the *Annales de la Propagation de la Foi*, will explain the circumstances preceding the persecution, and also the extreme facility with which almost all the missionaries fell into the hands of their enemies.

'At court,' writes M. Ridel, 'we had most powerful enemies. More than once they had demanded our death. They only awaited a favourable opportunity: it came, and they triumphed.

'Some Russian men-of-war, who appeared on the southern coast, demanded a concession of territory for the purposes of commerce; and great was the terror of the government.'

The prince regent felt the impossibility of much longer resisting the Russians, who had established themselves so near the Corea; and this request it appeared difficult to refuse. Under these circumstances, some Christians of noble birth, thinking that the intervention of the Vicar-apostolic would possibly save the government in this crisis, proposed to the prince regent and others that his mediation should be solicited. Monseigneur replied, when the question was formally put to him, that notwithstanding his willingness to be useful to the king—being neither of the same nation nor yet of the same religion as these Russians—it would be impossible that he should exercise any influence over them. He foresaw that, sooner or later, the Corea would be occupied by the Russians; but he abstained from blaming the policy which persisted in a refusal to treat with any European power.

Although the regent himself was not ill-disposed personally towards the Christian missionaries, he was under the influence of ministers who hated them. He therefore received coldly enough the memorial which the Christians had presented to him on this occasion; and this cold reception so terrified the author of it, Thomas Kim, that he took flight and hid himself.

The wife of the regent, who, by means of a Christian woman named Martha Pak, had for a long time been receiving instruction and advice from Mgr. Berneux, said to her one day: 'Why this inaction? The Russians will enter the Corea, and take possession of the country; whilst the Bishop, who might doubtless prevent this mischief, goes off to his mission in the interior, although we need him so much here. Let them write once more to my husband—it will succeed, I assure you—and then recall the Bishop.'

Martha at once reported the words of the queen to Thomas Hong, master of the house where Mgr. Berneux lived. A Christian mandarin, John Nam, was called in, and a second letter was written, which he carried himself to the regent, whom he found surrounded by his ministers, and who received him pretty favourably.

The following day the regent sent for him, and conversed for a long time with him upon the Christian religion. He acknowledged it all to be beautiful and true, remarking merely that he found one fault with it, inasmuch as it enjoined no sacrifices for the dead. At the conclusion of this interview, it was determined that the Vicar-apostolic should be sent for, in order that he might himself confer with the regent.

The report that the hour of religious emancipation had come spread at once everywhere. Thomas Kim came out of his hiding-place, and was surprised, on his return to Séoul, to find no one had been sent to call the Vicar-apostolic and his coadjutor, after this desire expressed by the regent. The reason assigned was the difficulty and the expense, for which money was needed, Mgr. Berneux being in the north, Mgr. Daveluy in the south of the country. This difficulty was at once obviated. Both money and carriages were supplied by the father-in-law of the regent's daughter; and Thomas Kim started off to find the Vicar-apostolic; whilst another Christian, Antony Ni, went to advertise the coadjutor.

Ten days after, Mgr. Daveluy arrived at Séoul, and four days later, Mgr. Berneux. This was the 29th of January. On the 31st John Nam presented himself before the regent, to give information concerning the arrival of the two Bishops. He was received coldly; and no desire was evinced to confer with the venerable prelates upon the subject for which they had been recalled.

This reception caused much disquiet. Nevertheless, but a few days before their arrest, a letter from Mgr. Berneux, written on the 10th of February, shows that up to this moment they were full of hope. 'I know not,' says he to M. Féron, 'whether or not in my last letter I have requested a Mass of you, for the peace of the kingdom and the happy conclusion of affairs. If I have not, I ask it now. It is the mother of the king who desires that each missionary should offer up a Mass for her intentions.

'I have a great desire to see you. It is now three years since I had this pleasure. This is too great a privation for us both. . . .

'I expected an interview with the regent, immediately after my return, since they sent for me in such haste; but until now he has said nothing. I think it will take place. Anyhow, a great step is gained. Let us pray our Lord and His Mother and ours to help me in these difficult circumstances; and recommend, above all, great circumspection to our Christians.'

Alas, far from liberty to the Christian Church— a fearful persecution was now about to fall like a thunderbolt upon the poor Christian mission of Corea.

A serious quarrel had arisen between the king and his family on one side, and the ministers on the other, in consequence of the false report of a persecution having broken out in China; and this brought about a catastrophe which can hardly be exaggerated for the Corean Church. It was the last drop which made their cup overflow. The ministers disapproved entirely of the proposal of their king, crying out loudly, 'Down with the Europeans! No alliance with them, or the independence of the kingdom is at an end!'

In the mean time, the Russians retired, the fears of the regent vanished; and he was weak enough to yield to the will of his ministers, and cruel enough to lend himself to their designs. The death of all the missionaries was instantly resolved upon.

Mgr. Berneux was then quietly awaiting the summons of the king to an interview, when, on the 14th of February, the soldiers presented themselves twice at the house he occupied, under pretext of collecting contributions towards the new palace which was being built by the regent. This double visit caused some disquiet in the mind of Thomas

Hong, the proprietor; and they sought, but in vain, another hiding-place for the articles most precious, and most likely to compromise the house. Mgr. Berneux refused to choose a safer retreat. He feared lest the search after him would bring on a general persecution. The good shepherd did not delude himself—he was ready to give his life for his sheep; too happy if his blood could assuage the thirst of his persecutors.

On the night of the 22d February, the satellites returned. They took a ladder, mounted the wall, and examined all the internal arrangements of the house. Alas! after all, the venerable prelate was betrayed, and by a servant in whom he had placed the greatest confidence. This faithless servant pointed out the dwelling of Mgr. Berneux, and furnished the ladder of which they made use. At four o'clock on the following afternoon, the house was surrounded by a numerous party. The satellites at once penetrated into the rooms occupied by the Vicar-apostolic; whom they seized, cruelly garrotted, and dragged away, without giving him time to put on his shoes. Six Christians were arrested with him; but in the tumult two others, and a child of eight years old, contrived to make their escape.

After having appeared before one of the judges of the capital, Mgr. Berneux was taken to the prison occupied by the worst malefactors. A few days after he was led to another of a less frightful description. On the 26th he was brought before all the ministers, and the following day before the regent, assisted by his son, and the four judges of the first tribunals of the kingdom. The following description of the judgment hall is from an eye-witness:

On one side of a spacious square court, a number of seats or tribunes are raised, upon which the judges sit. In the midst of this court is fixed a chair, upon which the accused is placed, with his face towards his judges. His feet are bound, his legs uncovered, his knees strongly fastened by cords to the seat upon which he is placed. The arms and shoulders are also pinioned in such a manner that, in spite of every torture, it is impossible for him to move. On either side, in double file, stand six or eight executioners, armed with instruments of punishment, which they will but too soon make use of. The scribe, whose business it is to take down the replies and the depositions of the accused and accusers, is seated a little farther back, and is hidden by a veil. Twenty-four soldiers, similarly armed, stand around, forming a semicircle facing the tribune of the judges. A larger number of soldiers is employed in holding back the crowd. As soon as the interrogatory begins, and during the whole time that the question or torture continues, the four-and-twenty soldiers make a heavy chanting noise, in order to cover the sound of the words and the moans of the sufferer. In Mgr. Berneux's case, two Christian soldiers assisted at his interrogatory, by whom the substance of his replies has been made known to us.

The first day his name and the time of his sojourn in the Corea were demanded; the reason of his coming, and whether he would consent to return to his native country. The holy Bishop replied that he had come to the Corea to work for the salvation of souls; and, in order to refute the calumnies of those who averred that the missionaries, being in want of the necessaries of life in their own country, had come to Corea in order to enrich themselves, he assured them that he had never received anything from the inhabitants, not even wood and water. 'If you take upon yourselves,' added he, 'to reconduct me to my own country, without doubt. I must go; but not otherwise. Do what you will; I am quite ready to give my life as a witness to the truth of the religion I have preached.'

The following day the interrogatory continued for a long time; but nothing to the prejudice of the Christians could be extracted from the lips of this venerable confessor of the faith. The tortures were applied, and they were most horrible. Our poor weak nature revolts at the bare recital of these torments. Nevertheless, some details must be given; for the longer and the more difficult the combat, the more glorious also has been the triumph of our holy martyrs; according to the beautiful thought of St. Ambrose: '*Non est gloriosa victoria nisi ubi fuerint laboriosa certamina.*'

The first torture was that of 'the plank.' This is the name of a long oak board, about five feet long by six inches wide and three inches thick, with which they strike violently the calf of the legs of the sufferer, tied as we have seen to the chair. Under their redoubled blows, the bones of the legs are soon bruised; and when the punishment ceases, it is necessary to wrap the wounds with oiled paper and pieces of linen, in order to reconduct the condemned one to prison. Another torture was that of striking successively every part of the body of the venerable prelate with pointed sticks thicker than one's arm. In a short time his whole body was but one mass of wounds and fractures.

After having been submitted many times to this frightful torture, Mgr. Berneux was quite exhausted, his voice became feeble, and the Christian soldiers who were present could no longer hear his replies to the numerous interrogatories which followed.

Three young missionaries, MM. de Bretenières, Beaulieu, and Dorié, were not long in sharing the captivity and the sufferings of their Vicar-apostolic. What a grand and touching scene was this! Our holy Bishop, bearing the weight of six-and-twenty years of apostolic labours, sinking under his trials, but finding strength enough to lead to martyrdom his three young companions; missionaries but one year in the Corea, and who seemed to have come there but to die!

The sentence of death was at last pronounced, and in these terms: 'Since (N.) refuses to obey, and will neither apostatise nor give the information required, nor yet return to his own country, he is sentenced to lose his head, after submitting to various other torments.'

On his return to prison, Mgr. Berneux was able to engage in conversation with his young companions in martyrdom, and with those Christians who had been arrested with him, and who were shortly to share his triumph. Thomas Hong, himself a captive, wrote two words to Mgr. Daveluy to this effect: 'Mgr. Berneux is always, and everywhere, full of dignity and holiness.'

On the 8th March 1866, Mgr. Berneux was led from prison to the place of execution. With him followed MM. de Bretenières, Beaulieu, and Dorié; and, a little after, Thomas Hong, and the mandarin John Nam. A crowd was collected near the prison, ready to heap insults upon the holy confessors. 'Do not rail or laugh in this way,' said Mgr. Berneux to them; 'for you have far more reason to weep! O, how you are to be pitied!' The thought of the loss of all hope for these unhappy people was the only thing which disturbed the peace of the saintly Bishop. Occasionally, during a halt, he would turn to his companions in order to say some word of encouragement; but more often he looked down upon the crowd which surrounded him, and with a sigh exclaimed, 'O, my God, how these poor heathen are to be pitied!'

These confessors for the faith were brought to the place of capital punishment reserved for the greatest criminals. It is situated on the banks of the river, about a league from the capital, and forms a vast sandy plain. A tent was erected for the mandarin whose duty it was to preside at the execution. Mgr. Berneux and his companions were each placed upon an enormous chair carried by two men: the legs were extended and bound as well as the arms; the head, slightly thrown back, was fixed by the hair. Above the chair, an inscription on wood asserted, 'N., rebel and disobedient; condemned to death after suffering various tortures.'

The soldiers and the executioners were arranged in the same order as before, the victims being in the centre of the semi-circle. The ligatures were then unfastened, and all their clothes but one slight covering removed. Mgr. Berneux, the glorious chief of this holy company of martyrs, had the honour of first entering the bloody arena. His arms were tied firmly behind his back, and an executioner seized each ear, transfixing it with an arrow, which remained there. Two others raised him by the arms upon two pieces of wood, making the round of the arena eight times, in such a manner that at the last they were left standing in the midst of it.

The moment for the last sacrifice, but also that of the supreme triumph, of our holy Bishop had now arrived. At a given signal, the eight executioners performed a savage dance all round their victim, who had fallen on his knees: his head fell forward, but was held back by the hair, which was tied to a cord in the hand of a soldier: they uttered loud cries, and directed their blows as seemed good to them. At the third cut, the head of Mgr. Berneux rolled upon the ground; and the soldiers as well as the executioners raised a loud yell of triumph, signifying that all was over.

The head, after having been presented to the mandarin, was suspended over the body, and the sentence of condemnation fixed above it, showing the name of the victim and the cause of his punishment.

The companions of Mgr. Berneux followed one by one. M. Dorié saw all this pass before his eyes before the consummation of his own glorious martyrdom. Their faithful neophytes were put to death the last.

MM. Petitnicolas and Pourthié had been unable to escape from their persecutors. On the 1st of March, nine satellites entered the St. John's College, and seized M. Pourthié; M. Petitnicolas awaited them at the open door. They were taken to the capital, and on the 11th March were decapitated; having first endured the same tortures and insults as their Bishop.

After the bodies of the first martyrs had remained for three days without sepulture, the inhabitants of the village of Sai-Namto received orders to bury them, and they were placed all together in one single grave near the place of execution. Towards the end of July, the persecution having a little abated, the Christians determined to give more honourable sepulture to these glorious victims of the faith, so that it might be possible one day to recognise them. It was with difficulty, however, that out of their poverty they found means to procure coffins for each of the martyrs. Some pious women gave their rings, the last ornaments they possessed, for this purpose: and on the 1st of August, forty Christians went secretly during the night to the place where the bodies had been buried; but their pious work was arrested by the dawn, and it was not until the 3d of August that they succeeded in carrying them all away, and in burying them, as much as possible according to the rites of the Church, upon a hill south of the capital. There they dug three graves in form of a triangle. In the first were placed the bodies of the Vicar-apostolic, M. de Bretenières and Ou Alexis, a young Corean of twenty-one years of age. In the second, MM. Pourthié, Petitnicolas; and in the third, MM. Beaulieu and Dorié. The inscriptions left inside each grave will facilitate the recovery of the remains of our glorious martyrs. At present they rest there, the precious seed which is destined to multiply a thousandfold the worshippers of the true God in this pagan land, awaiting the time when God will deign to glorify even here below, in the Church militant, these sacred Remains.

On the 30th of March, being Good Friday, of the year 1866, Mgr. Daveluy, M. l'Abbé Huin, and M. Aumaitre, went to join their martyred companions, leaving but three missionaries in the Corea, MM. Calais, Féron, and Ridel. These, after many and great dangers, succeeded in quitting the country in hopes of being able before long to return; but in 1867 M. Féron writes, 'The Corea has doubled and tripled its barriers, so that it is materially impossible to have any communication with our dear neophytes. Nevertheless we still hope to return, if events turn out as we anticipate, next spring.'

In the previous November 1866 M. Féron had written, 'Although the severest edicts have been published against the Christians, they have not been carried out. The mandarins themselves seek pretexts to elude them, and nearly every one has regretted the events of the month of March. But few Christians have been arrested, and I know only of three who have been beheaded since the 8th September, and four others who died of hunger at Kong-Tsiou.'

It is to be feared, however, that the intervention of France may redouble the persecution. Yet up to the present no news has come to justify this prediction. But were the persecution ten times more cruel, we know that the blood of martyrs can never flow in vain; and that God will at length have pity on this desolate Church. Tertullian assures us that the blood of martyrs is a fruitful seed; and St. John Chrysostom, completing this thought, tells us that the death of martyrs has a marvellous power—that it is a sermon which speaks not to the ears, but carries conviction to the very soul of the executioner. Everything in the East appears preparing for the future triumph of the Catholic faith. China is yielding more and more to commercial and European influence. Japan itself, so long and so firmly closed, acknowledges the utility of a connection with the West; and Corea, whose fate is inseparably united to that of China and Japan, will be unable eventually to resist this overwhelming influence; and thus we may safely predict a future for these far Eastern countries, resulting in the greater glory of our Lord, and in the salvation of the souls for whom He shed His precious Blood.

THE END.

www.ingramcontent.com/pod-product-compliance
Lightning Source LLC
Chambersburg PA
CBHW020256170426
43202CB00008B/399